Cookie Art

SWEET DESIGNS FOR SPECIAL OCCASIONS

Dear Melissa,

Thank you so much for supporting my work! I hope you enjoy this book!

♡ Amber Spiegel

Amber Spiegel of SweetAmbs®
Photos by Tom Moore

For my family.

Editors: Rebecca Freedman, Carolyn Mandarano, Tim Stobierski, Marc Schreibman
Copy Editor: Nina Rynd Whitnah
Indexer: Amber Spiegel
Cover and interior design: Alison Wilkes
Layout: Alison Wilkes
Photographer: Tom Moore
Prop & Wardrobe Stylist: Karen Donohue

Printed in the United States of America

Acknowledgments

Thank you to everyone who played a part in bringing this book to fruition:

My parents, for your unwavering support. Thank you for encouraging me to follow my dreams and for helping me to build a career out of cookies and icing.

Marc, for being by my side and sharing in my enthusiasm for this craft. Thank you for giving me the confidence to keep climbing.

To Grandma Jewel, for continuing to inspire me with your sense of style. Thank you for always being my cheerleader and my number one fan!

Tom Moore, for bringing your incredible talent to the table. Capturing every photo using only natural light in mid-November was an incredible feat!

Karen Donohue, for going above and beyond to style the shots for this book. Your eye for detail and dedication to the project enhanced the beauty of every cookie.

Alison Wilkes and Shawna Mullen for opening this door to me. Thank you for your guidance in getting this project off the ground.

Rosalind Wanke for your design expertise and ensuring that every shot was just right. Timothy Stobierski, Rebecca Freedman, and Nina Whitnah, for your sharp eyes and all of the hours of hard work that you each put into making this book a reality.

The chef instructors at The Culinary Institute of America for expecting nothing less than perfection from your students.

To my own students, online and in-person, whose passion for cookie decorating motivates and inspires me to never stop creating.

My brothers, Emmet and Garrett, for generously offering your time to help me in the studio, and just for being who you are.

To my friends near and far, for always being there for me, whether to lend a hand or lend an ear. Your support means the world to me!

Contents

Introduction

GROWING UP IN A SMALL TOWN IN UPSTATE NEW YORK SURROUNDED BY AN ARTISTIC family, I spent a lot of my free time with a colored pencil, marker, or paintbrush in my hand. I've also had a sweet tooth for as long as I can remember, which always kept me busy in the kitchen experimenting with dessert recipes. After my first serious attempt at decorating cookies in 2007, I'd never imagined that I'd create a business around decorating cookies. I haven't stopped creating cookie art since that first batch and what started out as a part-time hobby has turned into a full-time career.

Before I started my cookie decorating business, SweetAmbs® (short for Sweet Amber) I'd always envisioned myself with a full service bakery with muffins, cakes, donuts and all kinds of baked goods. However, soon after I graduated from culinary school with a degree in baking and pastry arts, I realized that the reality of running a high-volume production establishment was definitely not for me! It became clear that I enjoyed decorating with icing and fondant much more than baking, which led me down the path of becoming a cookie artist. Cookies have become the perfect medium for me to combine my artistic skills with my love of all things sweet. Just one batch of delicious Orange Vanilla Spice cookie dough gives me a few dozen blank canvases ready to be decorated. The possibilities are endless! And, if I don't like a design I made on one cookie, I can put it aside and start on a new one! It has been a great way to develop my creativity with icing.

One of the best things about making decorated cookies is that because royal icing (the icing that will be used throughout this book) dries hard, you can make such icing decorations as piped roses several weeks ahead of time and apply them to your cookies later. That way, you won't be trying to make your cookie dough, mix your icing, and decorate the cookies all at once. It takes a lot of the stress off when you can break a big project up into small steps. And, if you need something pretty in a pinch, you can use these pre-made icing decorations to add a beautiful, handmade touch to other desserts, such as store bought cupcakes or even boxed brownies.

Another reason I love decorated cookies is that they make great gifts! Since royal icing dries hard, your cookies can be wrapped up in a box and shipped across oceans to be enjoyed by others. If the cookies are wrapped carefully, there are no worries about your decorations being smudged or smashed along the way.

The projects I've shared here are meant to inspire you to create your own amazing edible treats. While you browse through these designs, keep in mind that cookie decorating takes patience and requires some planning ahead. It's also very important to remember that you will get better with practice! Don't get discouraged if your cookies don't come out the way you want them to right away. We all have to start somewhere! Even after decorating thousands of cookies, I still have plenty of moments where I look down at a set of cookies I just spent hours making and I think, this is terrible! It's in those moments when I have to step away from the cookies and take a little break. When I come back and look at my "terrible" cookies, I realize that they aren't half bad! And, of course, the recipient is always impressed. So, don't be too hard on yourself. Cookie decorating should be a relaxing activity, so get creative with the techniques that you find in this book and have lots of fun!

{ PART ONE }

GETTING STARTED

{ 1 }

TOOLS & TECHNIQUES

TO MAKE A BEAUTIFUL COOKIE, YOU HAVE TO START WITH THE BASICS, and of course, you also need the right tools for the job. In this chapter, I've shared my favorite decorating tools and techniques for everything from making a perfectly smooth icing base to adding gorgeous detail to your cookies. With a little bit of practice and patience, you'll learn techniques in this chapter that will help you create impressive edible works of art to share with your friends and family.

Baking Tools

These are the tools that I use for all of my cookie designs, in some form or other. With the tools listed here, you can create any of the cookies in this book.

1. Aluminum baking sheet

Before I spent time working in commercial bakeries, I'd go out and try to find the fanciest cookie sheets that boasted the best baking results. Since then, I've learned that all I need to bake my cookies is a simple aluminum, rimmed, baking sheet lined with parchment paper. You don't need to be a professional baker to find these inexpensive pans online or in restaurant supply stores. I prefer the half-sheet size, about 18 by 13 inches.

2. Rubber spatula

When making cookie dough or royal icing, you'll need this sturdy tool to scrape the bowl. The rubber spatula is useful for getting into the crevices in the paddle attachment and getting down to the bottom of the bowl underneath the paddle attachment.

3. Bowl scraper

To make sure that you get every bit of dough out of the bottom of the bowl, I recommend using a flexible bowl scraper. The bowl scraper gives you more leverage than the rubber spatula for this task.

4. Cookie cutters

Most of my cookie designs are made on round or square cookies. I use a nesting cookie cutter set that includes circles ranging from 7/8 inch to 4 inches in diameter, as well as a T-square ruler with a paring knife to cut out squares. Once in a while,

however, I come across a cookie cutter shape that I can't live without. The copper fancy plaque, for example, is one of my favorites.

5. T-square

When making square or rectangle cookies, I use a T-square ruler to create perfectly straight edges and 90 degree angles. A T-square ruler can be found at an office supply store or at a craft store in the art supply section. I purchased mine at the craft store.

6. Paring knife

When you need a cookie in a particular shape and you don't have the right cutter, you can make your own template out of cardstock and cut around it with this knife. I also use my paring knife for splitting vanilla beans.

7. Citrus Zester

If I need to straighten the edges of my cookies, I file them with a citrus zester, such as the Microplane® brand zester. (It's important to have very straight edges on the cookies when you're making a cookie box, for example.) Of course, I use this tool to zest citrus for my cookie dough, too!

8. Marble rolling pin

I prefer a heavy marble one; its weight makes it much easier to roll out chilled dough. I don't think I'll ever go back to using a wooden pin!

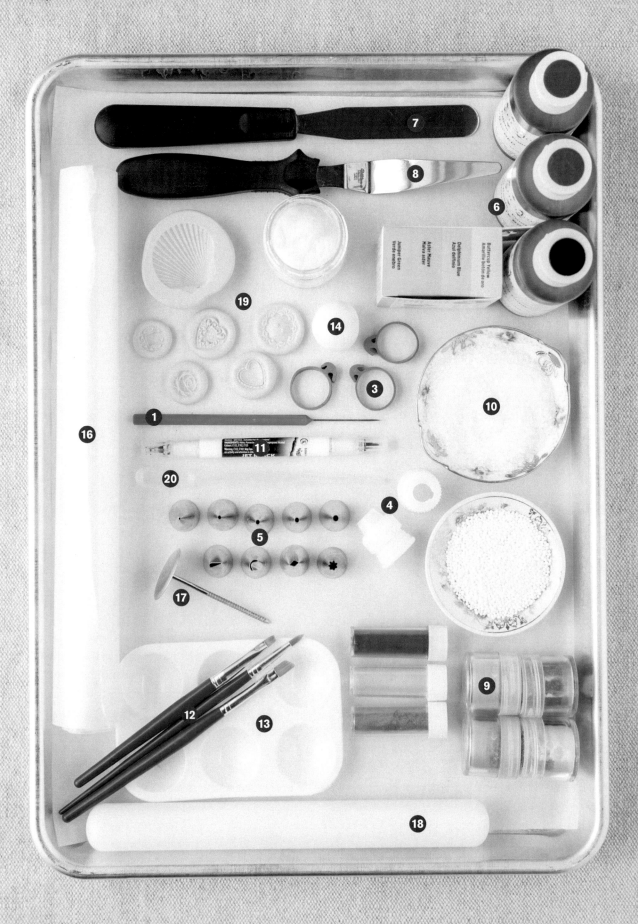

Decorating Tools

1. Scribe tool

This tool is by far my favorite because it's so versatile. I use it to help with flooding, to create small details, to draw guides on the icing before I add details, and even to help correct mistakes. A suitable substitute could be an awl tool or, in some cases, toothpick.

2. 12-inch pastry bags

This size bag is the perfect size for cookie decorating. You can use reusable or disposable plastic bags, depending on your preference.

3. Bag ties

These keep the back of the pastry bag closed tightly so that icing doesn't drip out everywhere. They also prevent the icing from drying in the bag and flaking off onto your decorated cookies. I prefer a bag tie to a rubber band because the little tab on the end makes it a cinch to close.

4. Couplers

A coupler is two-piece plastic adaptor that is used to attach a decorating tip to a pastry bag. They make it really easy to switch tips or remove a tip to clean it if it gets clogged.

5. Tips

The tips that I use most often for decorating cookies are Wilton® tips 1, 2, 3, 4, 5, and 8. Even for the tiniest details, I don't normally use anything smaller than a tip 1. By changing the pressure on my icing bag, I'm able to make very thin lines.

6. Gel pastes

A type of food coloring that's ideal for royal icing, gel paste is concentrated so that you don't have to use too much of it at once. Its low water content keeps it from affecting the consistency of the icing.

7. 9-inch flat metal spatula

I use this tool for mixing icing while thinning it down and adding color. A metal spatula is sturdy and easily wipes clean between colors.

8. 9-inch offset metal spatula

If I'm using color from a jar rather than a squeeze bottle, I use a small offset spatula for scooping out the gel paste and adding it to my icing. Like the flat spatula, the offset spatula is easy to wipe clean. This tool is also great for scraping icing off a cookie if you've made a mistake, and for helping remove dry royal icing transfers from waxed paper.

9. Pearl dusts

I have a bit of an addiction to edible pearl dusts, which are used to add sparkle and shine to decorated cookies; there's a drawer full of different brands and colors in my studio. Used dry and brushed onto cookies, pearl dusts add a little bit of shimmer; mixed with vodka or flavored extract, they can be used as paint for a more brilliant shine. From time to time, I also use matte dusts to add just a little bit of color. Some of my favorites dusts are made by Crystal Colors® and Wilton®.

10. Sprinkles and sparkling sugars

Sprinkles and sparkling sugars are a quick and easy way to add interest and dimension to your cookies. Not only do they come in a variety of colors, but you can also find them in all sorts of shapes and sizes.

11. Edible ink markers

Edible ink markers are great for drawing guides on a bare cookie or dry royal icing when it's not practical to pipe a freehand design. I'll show you later in this book how to use edible ink markers to draw guides for piping. You can also use them to draw tiny details! My favorite edible markers are made by FooDoodler® and Rainbow Dust.

12. Brushes

The three brush shapes used most often throughout this book are round, square, and flat angled, which are available in a set from Wilton®. I also recommend having a soft mop brush for dusting and a very fine tip brush for small details; you can find these in the artist brush section of a craft store.

13. Paint palette

A palette like this one can be found in the art supply section of craft stores. The small wells are perfect for mixing up gel pastes or pearl dusts for painting. If you don't have a paint palette, you can use small dishes instead.

14. Fondant

Pliable sugar dough that can be shaped and molded into almost anything, fondant allows you to quickly create an intricate design using a flexible mold or even something very delicate, such as a paper thin rose petal, both of which I will show you how to do later in this chapter.

15. Gum paste mat

This mat has a clear plastic flap that keeps fondant and gum paste from drying out after you've rolled it into a thin sheet.

16. Wax paper

It's best to use wax paper when making royal icing transfers or piped roses (see p. 22 and 24). Royal icing peels off wax paper easily, and it doesn't wrinkle as much as parchment when it comes in contact with moisture. This will ensure that your royal icing transfers dry smooth and flat.

17. Flower nail

A flower nail acts as a tiny turntable that is held between your thumb and forefinger as you create a piped rose. Using this tool keeps the rose in a position that makes it easier to pipe the petals. Piping the petals while simultaneously turning the flower nail keeps the petals evenly spaced all the way around. See p. 24 for the tutorial on how to make a piped rose.

18. Fondant rolling pin

Small and plastic, this tool is perfect for rolling out small amounts of fondant or gum paste.

19. Flexible molds

Fondant can be turned into almost any kind of decoration with a flexible mold. You can find a virtually endless variety of shapes online, or you can make your own, as I did with a food-safe mold-making material. You can find it online or at the craft store (I purchase mine from Michaels® craft store). It's so much fun to collect buttons, cameos, and other little trinkets for mold making!

20. Eyedropper

This is a handy tool when you just need a tiny bit of liquid. I use an eyedropper to add liquid when painting with gel paste or pearl dust.

21. Cake board

These greaseproof pieces of cardboard come in several shapes and sizes. You can find them in the cake-decorating aisle of the craft store or online. I find them useful for practicing piping and holding royal icing transfers, as described on p. 22

21. Acrylic sheet

Flat, smooth, portable and resistant to warping, an acrylic sheet (such as Plexiglas®) is the best surface on which to pipe royal icing transfers (p. 22).

Royal Icing Consistencies

Stiff Consistency Royal Icing

My royal icing recipe on p. 124 has a stiff consistency; it's thick, dense, has a dull finish, and holds a stiff peak. It's best to beat it on medium-low speed in a stand mixer fitted with the paddle attachment for no more than 5 minutes. If you beat it on high speed or for too long and your icing becomes fluffy, later on it will lead to problems, such as air bubbles. For some tips on troubleshooting your royal icing, see p. 129. Stiff consistency icing is used for decorations that need to hold shape and definition, such as piped roses, brush embroidery, basket weave, and shell borders.

At this point, you can alter the consistency of the icing to make medium or flood consistency. Place the icing into a separate container for each consistency that you will be making. It's a good idea to always keep some stiff consistency icing on hand in case you accidentally add too much water when thinning it down. I'll explain more about that in a moment.

Medium Consistency Royal Icing

Medium consistency icing is what some refer to as piping consistency. It flows out the tip very smoothly, but can also hold its shape well. This consistency is best for decorations such as filigree, double bead borders, monograms, and piping script. To make medium consistency icing, add about a teaspoon of water at a time to stiff consistency icing until it holds a very soft peak and has a shiny finish.

Flood Consistency Royal Icing

Flood consistency icing is used to create a smooth, blank canvas on which to decorate. It's also used for the wet-on-wet technique, which I'll show you on p. 18. This is one of the most difficult consistencies to get right, so don't feel discouraged if it doesn't work the first time. To make flood consistency icing, add water, a few teaspoons at a time, to stiff consistency icing until it takes 15 to 20 seconds for the icing to smooth itself out. To test this, scoop a spoonful of icing from the bowl and immediately drop it back in. It should take 15 to 20 seconds for it to completely disappear back into the rest of the icing. If your icing is too watery, add a scoop of stiff icing to thicken it up rather than just adding confectioners' sugar, or you'll upset the ratio of confectioners' sugar to meringue powder. There's more on that in the Royal Icing Troubleshooting Tips section of this book.

Stiff Medium Flood

Coloring Icing

For royal icing, it's best to use a coloring that's concentrated and has a low moisture content, such as a gel paste, so that the consistency of the icing isn't affected. Also, a concentrated coloring lets you add less to achieve the desired shade.

To add color to the icing, I prefer to use a tapered offset spatula, but a toothpick works just fine, too. Even if I'm using a squeeze bottle of color, I squeeze the color out onto the spatula and then dip it into the icing so that I don't accidentally add too much at once.

I usually mix my icing colors in pint-size containers by hand, but if I'm making a large batch of cookies (4 dozen or more), I'll color an entire batch of icing in the mixing bowl of my stand mixer and let the paddle do the work.

The colors I use most often come from the Wilton® Garden Color set, which yield the antique shades used on the cookies throughout this book. This set comes with four colors: Delphinium Blue, Aster Mauve, Juniper Green, and Buttercup Yellow. You can also achieve these antique-looking shades by adding a touch of black to pinks, blues, and greens, which gives them a "dusty" look.

When you're mixing up a dark color such as black, red or brown, use the smallest amount of coloring possible to achieve the desired shade. All colors will darken over time, so to be absolutely sure that you'll have the right shade, it's best to let the icing sit for at least an hour. When I want black icing, I add just enough color to make the icing dark gray, and then let it sit to darken on its own. If you need a medium shade of blue, make it a little bit lighter than you want it so that you don't end up with dark blue cookies later.

If you have to decorate several cookies using one particular color, make enough of that shade the first time so that you don't have to try to match it later. It's likely that no one will notice if there are two ever-so-slightly different colors in your set of cookies, but keep in mind that it's nearly impossible to make the same exact shade of icing twice.

How to Color Icing

Choosing a color palette for your project is one of the first steps in creating a gorgeous set of cookies. I find color inspiration in antique and vintage pieces, such as fabrics, tea sets, and even greeting cards.

YOU'LL NEED

Tapered offset spatula
or toothpick

Gel paste food coloring

Royal icing (any consistency)

Straight 9-inch metal
or small rubber spatula

1. Separate the icing into separate containers for each color that you will make. Keep the containers of icing that you're not working with at the moment tightly covered so that the icing doesn't dry out.

2. Dip the tapered offset spatula or toothpick into the jar of coloring (or squeeze a bit of color onto the spatula), and then dip the spatula into the icing. Using a straight 9-inch metal spatula or a small rubber spatula, thoroughly mix the color into the icing. Be sure to add a small amount of coloring at a time; it's easier to make the icing darker than it is to lighten it back up. If you do accidentally add too much color, you can mix in more white icing to lighten the batch.

MAKING BROWN ICING

I find that a lot of brown gel pastes look pink on their own, so I almost always add a drop of Juniper Green to tone down the pink, which helps the icing look truly brown.

How to Fill a Pastry Bag

Knowing the basics of how to fill a pastry bag is key to having a mess-free (and stress-free) decorating session!

YOU'LL NEED

12-inch pastry bag

Coupler

Piping tip

Royal icing (any consistency)

Bag tie

1. Before you fill your pastry bag with icing, you'll have to prep it with a coupler and a piping tip. Unscrew the cap of the coupler from the larger piece and drop the larger piece into the bag. Push it all the way to the end of the bag so that the plastic is snug around it. Using a scissor, make a mark on the first groove of the coupler, closest to the tip. Move the coupler out of the way and trim the bag on the mark that you just made. Push the coupler back to the end of the bag, place the piping tip over the coupler on the outside of the bag, and screw on the cap. If the tip feels loose or moves around, try changing caps on the coupler. (If you have old and new couplers mixed up, the pieces might not always fit together properly.)

2. To prevent the icing from leaking from the tip when you fill the bag, twist the bag right above the coupler and push the twisted plastic into the back end of the tip, which acts as a temporary plug. To fill the bag, cuff the plastic around your hand to create a well. Spoon 4 or 5 spoonfuls of icing into the bag, making sure not to overfill it. (I usually fill mine less than halfway.) If the bag is too full, it will be hard to control the flow when you pipe.

3. Close the top of the bag with a bag tie. Fold the bag in half and put it in an empty cup or container with the tip facing up; this will keep the icing from leaking out or clogging the tip.

4. When you're ready to decorate, hold the pastry bag so that you have just a handful of icing in your hand. The rest of the icing will sit behind your hand, held in by the bag tie. Place one or two fingers on the tip or above the tip to help steady the bag as you pipe.

PASTRY BAG SHORT CUT

I don't always use a coupler in my pastry bags. I'll skip it if I'm not going to need to change the tip on my pastry bag while working on a particular project. To work without a coupler, trim about 1 inch from the end of the bag and drop the tip in.

Push it to the end of the bag and gently stretch the plastic around the back end of the tip, creating a seal, so that the icing doesn't leak out around the tip.

HOW TO ICE A COOKIE

The flooding technique for icing a cookie creates a perfectly smooth surface on which to decorate. I prefer to outline and fill in my cookies with flood consistency royal icing rather than outlining in a stiff consistency icing first; this saves time, allowing me to make icing in just one consistency instead of two. I also love this method because it doesn't require me to pipe a perfect circle. Instead, I can use the scribe tool to shape the icing after I've iced the cookie.

YOU'LL NEED

12-inch pastry bag

Number 3 piping tip

Un-iced cookie

Flood consistency royal icing

Bag tie

Scribe tool or toothpick

1. Fit the pastry bag with a number 3 piping tip. Fill the bag with icing. Hold the tip slightly above the surface of the cookie at a 90 degree angle. Start about ¼ inch in from the edge of the cookie and pipe an outline. It doesn't have to be perfect! You'll be able to fix it in a moment.

2. Using a spiral motion as you work toward the center, immediately fill in the cookie. It's okay if you have a few gaps in the icing.

3. Hold the scribe tool (or a toothpick) like a pencil, and with a swirling motion, use it to evenly distribute the icing and push it toward the edge of the cookie, filling in any gaps along the way. Try not to scratch the surface of the cookie too much during this process. Continue pushing the icing out until you have about ⅛ inch of space all the way around the edge of the cookie.

4. Let the icing dry for 4 hours before adding any more decoration and until completely dry, at least 8 hours, before packaging. I recommend that you place the cookies in front of a fan for at least the first hour to help the drying process. You can read more about this on p. 129.

FLOOD ICING TIPS

Rotate the cookie while you use the scribe tool to push the icing out toward the edge. This will help to keep the icing even all the way around. Keep in mind that the icing will start to crust over within about 5 minutes, so try to work quickly. If the icing is bumpy when you're finished, gently tap the cookie on the table a few times to smooth it out. If your icing is too thin and starting to run off the edges, use a tapered metal spatula to remove some of the icing from the cookie. In this case, you might have to thicken your icing. Read the Royal Icing Troubleshooting Tips on p. 129 for more information.

Wet-on-Wet Technique

The wet-on-wet technique involves icing a cookie and then immediately adding decoration in flood consistency icing so that the design is flat and smooth. Keep in mind that flood consistency icing will begin to crust over within about 5 minutes, so you'll have to work rather quickly. Make sure to have all of the pastry bags filled and ready to go before you begin any of these wet-on-wet designs.

ROSES

This wet-on-wet rose is one of my very favorite techniques. All it takes is a few swirls of icing to create an impressive design.

YOU'LL NEED

12-inch pastry bag fitted with a number 3 piping tip and filled with white flood consistency royal icing

12-inch pastry bag fitted with a number 2 piping tip and filled with light pink flood consistency royal icing

12-inch pastry bag fitted with a number 1 piping tip and filled with dark pink flood consistency royal icing

12-inch pastry bag fitted with a number 1 piping tip and filled with light green flood consistency royal icing

12-inch pastry bag fitted with a number 1 piping tip and filled with dark green flood consistency royal icing

Un-iced cookie

Scribe tool or toothpick

COLORS

Light and dark pink = Wilton® Aster Mauve

Light and dark green = Wilton® Juniper Green

1. Ice a cookie with white flood consistency royal icing. With the light pink flood consistency royal icing, pipe an oval slightly above the center of the cookie. Pipe a letter "G" in the center of the oval using the dark pink flood consistency royal icing.

2. Using the scribe tool, make a small swirl slightly above the center of the G in the oval. The swirl will become the central cluster of petals in your rose design.

3. With wide sweeping motions, drag the scribe tool back and forth through the icing, making sure to feather the edges. Be careful to not disturb the small swirl that you made in step 2.

4. Pipe a dot of dark green flood consistency royal icing followed by a smaller dot of light green and another dot of dark green for each leaf. Pull the scribe tool through the icing to create a leaf shape.

DOTS

Wet-on-wet dots are an easy way to create an adorable background for nearly any cookie design. Try a combination of light blue icing with white dots for a baby shower cookie, or pink icing with red dots for Valentine's Day!

YOU'LL NEED

12-inch pastry bag fitted with a number 3 piping tip and filled with flood consistency royal icing

12-inch pastry bag fitted with a number 1 piping tip and filled flood consistency royal icing in a different color.

Un-iced cookie

Scribe tool or toothpick

1. Ice the cookie with flood consistency royal icing and number 3 tip. Use the scribe tool to evenly distribute the icing as described in the flooding technique on p. 17.

2. With flood consistency icing in a different color and a number 1 tip, immediately add a row of 4 evenly spaced dots down the middle of the cookie, holding the tip at a 90 degree angle and slightly hovering above the surface. Pipe staggered dots on both sides of the center row and continue until you reach the edges of the cookie.

MARBLING

You can use as many colors as you'd like for this technique. Try dragging the icing in all different directions for unique variations in the design.

YOU'LL NEED

12-inch pastry bag fitted with a number 3 piping tip and filled with flood consistency royal icing

12-inch pastry bags fitted with a number 1 piping tip and filled with flood consistency royal icing in different colors

Flood consistency icing

Un-iced cookie

Scribe tool or toothpick

1. Ice the cookie with flood consistency royal icing and number 3 tip. Pipe stripes of two or more different colors of flood consistency royal icing and number 1 tip.

2. Drag a scribe tool or toothpick vertically through the horizontal stripes. Wipe the scribe tool clean of excess icing in between swipes.

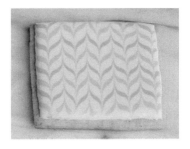

3. Drag the scribe tool back through the stripes in the opposite direction in the spaces between the first dragged rows.

QUILTING

Use this technique for a puffy pillow effect! This method is great for making baby quilts and even pumpkin decorations. Try alternating between two or more colors for a fun variation on this technique!

YOU'LL NEED

Un-iced cookie

Edible ink marker

Ruler

12-inch pastry bag fitted with a number 2 piping tip and filled with flood consistency royal icing

Scribe tool or toothick

1. Draw a 1-inch diamond pattern on the cookie using an edible ink marker and a ruler.

2. Fill in every other square with icing, making sure that the corners are just barely touching. Use the scribe tool to help evenly distribute the icing within the squares as described in the flooding technique. Allow the icing to dry about 1 hour.

3. Fill in the remaining squares and let the icing dry completely.

QUICK TIP

Use a flexible plastic ruler so that it sits flush against the surface of the cookie. You can make your own flexible ruler by marking 1- inch increments on a strip of construction paper.

PATTERN TRANSFER

If you don't own a cake projector (a tool that projects an image onto a cake or cookie so that you can trace it) but need a way to make an exact copy of an image or text on a cookie, this method is perfect. I call this technique the "tissue paper method," because it uses tissue paper that you'd find in a gift bag.

YOU'LL NEED

1 sheet of tissue paper

Image of your choice, printed on a piece of paper (the filigree template is on p. 134)

Edible ink marker (I use Rainbow Dust brand here because it has a very fine tip)

Completely dry iced cookie (see p. 17 for instructions)

1. Place a piece of tissue paper over the image that you want to transfer. Use a copy of an image that you don't mind getting dirty, because the ink will mark it up.

2. Use an edible ink marker to trace the image.

3. Move the tissue paper onto the cookie and trace over it again with the edible ink marker.

4. Before removing the tissue paper, lift a corner to make sure that the ink has bled through the paper onto the icing.

5. Allow the ink to dry for a couple of minutes. You're now ready to pipe over the design.

QUICK TIP

If you accidentally make a mark where you don't want it with the edible ink marker, use a scribe tool to scratch it off or use a slightly damp brush to wash it away.

Royal Icing Transfers

A royal icing transfer is a design that's piped onto a piece of wax paper, allowed to dry, and then peeled off and transferred onto a cookie. If you plan ahead, royal icing transfers can save you a lot of time. Make them several weeks in advance, store them in an airtight container at room temperature, and use them when you're ready to decorate your cookies. They're also great for dressing up other desserts. Keep some royal icing transfers on hand to make an impressive dessert when you're in a pinch. (For more information, see the Pretty Pastries section in chapter 7).

YOU'LL NEED

Template (see p. 137)

Cake board, baking sheet, or other hard surface such as a Plexiglas® board

Masking tape

Wax paper

Flood or medium consistency icing

12-inch pastry bag

Number 1, 2, or 3 piping tip, depending on the size of the design

Bag tie

Scribe tool or toothpick

1. Place the template on a cake board, baking sheet, or Plexiglas® board, and secure it with tape. Place a sheet of wax paper over the board and secure that with tape as well.

2. Fit a pastry bag with a piping tip, fill the bag with flood or medium consistency royal icing, depending on what type of design you're making. (If your design has a large surface area, such as the bird shown on p. 50, it's best to work with flood consistency icing. If you're making a small delicate design such as a tea pot, it's best to use medium consistency so that you don't lose the tiny details as you pipe.) Pipe over the template.

3. Let the icing dry completely, 8 to 12 hours. You can put the transfers in front of a fan for at least the first hour to help them dry, but be sure that the fan doesn't blow the edge of the paper upwards. That might break your transfers!

4. When the transfers are dry, slide a knife under the wax paper to slice the edge and loosen it from the board.

5. Gently peel the paper from the transfers and store them in an airtight container for later use, or apply them directly to an iced cookie. It's best to place the transfer onto the cookie just after it has been iced, so that the transfer can sink slightly into the icing. That way, there won't be any gaps under the transfer, which could lead to breakage. If you're having trouble with fragile transfers or color bleed when applying transfers to wet icing, refer to the section on Royal Icing Troubleshooting Tips on p.129.

Brush Embroidery

I first saw this technique used on a wedding cake during my studies at The Culinary Institute of America, and I was completely baffled about how icing could look so much like fabric! A classmate explained the method to me, but it wasn't until after I graduated that I tried it myself on a birthday cake I made for my mom. It has since become one of my favorite decorating techniques.

YOU'LL NEED

12-inch pastry bag

Number 2 or 3 piping tip

Stiff consistency royal icing

Bag tie

Completely dry iced cookie (see p. 17 for instructions)

Square tip brush

Small dish of water

Dry paper towel

1. Fit a pastry bag with a number 2 or 3 piping tip and fill the bag with stiff consistency royal icing. I like to make my brush embroidered decorations with a ruffled edge. To do this, begin by touching the tip to the surface of the iced cookie at a 45 degree angle. While squeezing the bag, lift the tip up so that it is hovering above the surface and allow the icing to fall slightly forward (away from you) onto the surface. Then touch the tip to the surface again. Continue to pipe with an up-and-down motion to create small hills with the icing.

2. Dip the square tip brush into the dish of water and dab it on a dry paper towel to remove the excess. The brush should be slightly damp.

3. Using the edge of the brush, drag the icing toward you. Continue to drag the icing by using the edge of the brush, until the entire line of icing is brushed.

BRUSH EMBROIDERY TIPS

Work with small sections of icing at a time. If you pipe the entire design all at once, it will be too dry to brush it. Make sure your brush is not too wet. If you have water pooling on the cookie, dab it with a dry paper towel to soak up the excess water.

PIPED ROSES

Piping roses might be a challenge at first, but once you get the hang of it, you won't want to stop! These decorations are a great way to dress up a cookie, cake, or cupcake. Take a look at the Pretty Pastries section in chapter 7 for other ways to use these make-ahead decorations. Use a piping tip 59s for a small rose with curved petals, or use a bigger tip, such as a number 104, to make a larger rose. In this tutorial, I'll be using a piping tip number 101. Use this technique with the buttercream frosting recipe from p. 125 for a quick decoration for cupcakes, cakes, or brownies.

YOU'LL NEED

12-inch pastry bag fitted with a number 101 petal piping tip and filled with stiff consistency royal icing

Small squares of wax paper (about 1.5x1.5 inch)

Number 6 flower nail

12-inch pastry bag fitted with a number 352 leaf piping tip and filled with stiff consistency royal icing

QUICK TIP

Make sure to keep the tip close to the center of the rose while piping the petals. This will keep the flower tight and compact.

1. Attach a square of wax paper to a number 6 flower nail with a dab of icing.

2. Pipe a mound of icing in the center of the paper. This will be the base of the rose.

3. Position the tip so that the wide end is down and the narrow end is up. Angle the narrow end of the tip slightly in toward the center. Touch the wide end of the tip to the base of the icing mound. While twirling the nail between your fingers, squeeze the bag and pull it toward you to wrap the icing all the way around the center mound to create a bud.

4. Touch the wide end of the tip to the bud. Keep the narrow end of the tip angled in toward the center. Squeeze and lift the tip and bring it back down to create an arc with the icing. Touch the tip to the bud again at the bottom of the arc and stop squeezing before you pull the tip away. Repeat this process twice more to make a total of 3 petals, making sure to slightly overlap the petals.

5. Pipe 5 outer petals using the same motion used to make the inner petals, but angle the narrow end of the tip slightly out so that it points away from the center. You can switch to a lighter shade of icing for the outer petals to create a two-tone rose.

6. Gently slide the paper off the nail and allow the flower to dry completely, about 4 hours.

7. To make leaves, fit a pastry bag with a number 352 leaf piping tip and fill the bag with green stiff consistency royal icing. Place the tip at the base of the rose and hold it in place while you squeeze, allowing the icing to build up around the tip before pulling it away. Make sure to stop squeezing before pulling away so that the leaf does not become too elongated.

Fondant

This sweet pliable icing can be used in a variety of ways. I like to add small fondant decorations to my royal icing covered cookies for an elegant touch.

MOLDED FONDANT

Using fondant molds is a quick and easy way to make a beautiful decoration. I like to make my own molds using food-safe mold-making material with trinkets and buttons that I've collected over the years. If you don't want to make your own mold, you can search for pre-made molds online.

1. Dust the inside of the mold with a little bit of cornstarch to prevent the fondant from sticking.

2. Press the fondant into the mold, making sure to press hard enough so that the fondant fills all of the little crevices.

3. Bend the mold backwards and use the scribe tool to help push the fondant out of the mold.

4. Apply the decoration to a cookie right away, or allow it to dry overnight and store it in an airtight container for later use.

YOU'LL NEED

Flexible mold

Cornstarch

1-inch ball of fondant

Scribe tool or toothpick

DRESS IT UP!

Molded fondant decorations can be made several weeks ahead and applied to dry or wet royal icing when it's time to decorate your cookies.

FONDANT ROSE PETAL

A realistic looking edible rose petal makes a gorgeous decoration for cookies. You can also use them to dress up other desserts like brownies or cupcakes.

YOU'LL NEED

Vegetable shortening

Gum paste mat

Fondant

Fondant rolling pin

Small round cookie cutter, approximately 7/8 inch

Offset spatula

Baking sheet

Parchment paper

Cornstarch

Flat angled brush

Pink pearl dust, such as Crystal Colors™ Blush Gold or Wilton® Orchid Pink

Round brush

Gold pearl dust, such as Wilton® Gold or Crystal Colors™ Antique Gold

1. Apply a thin layer of vegetable shortening to a gum paste mat by hand. Place a small piece of white fondant under the flap and using the fondant rolling pin, roll it to about 1/16-inch thick.

2. Cut circles with the small round cookie cutter. Move one circle to an empty portion of the mat.

3. With the flap closed, use your finger to thin the edges of the fondant, while shaping the circle into a rose petal shape. Widen the circle at the top and bring the bottom to a point.

4. Use an offset spatula to help remove the rose petal from the gum paste mat. Transfer the petal to a parchment-lined baking sheet dusted with cornstarch to dry overnight.

5. Use a flat angled brush to apply dry pink pearl dust to the top edge of the rose petal. Use a round brush to apply gold pearl dust to the point.

QUICK TIP

To curl the petal, lay a jar of gel paste food coloring (or any small cylindrical item) on its side, dust it with cornstarch, and place the petal on it to dry.

PAINTING

Painting on royal icing might seem intimidating at first, but once you give it a try, you won't want to put that brush down! When painting with pearl dust or gel paste food coloring, it's best to use a liquid with high alcohol content. Alcohol evaporates quickly, so it's less likely to dissolve the royal icing as you're painting. I prefer to use vodka for this method, but vanilla or lemon extract also work well.

YOU'LL NEED

Completely dry iced cookie (see p. 17 for instructions)

Offset tapered spatula

Gel paste food coloring

Palette or small dish

Alcohol or flavored extract

Round brush

Dry paper towel

Dish of water

1. With the offset tapered spatula, scoop a small amount of gel paste (about 1/8 tsp.) into paint palette or small dish. Use an eyedropper to add a few drops of alcohol or flavored extract to create an edible watercolor paint. Start out with 3 to 4 drops and add more if your paint seems thick and chunky.

2. With the round brush, test the color on a dry paper towel before painting the cookie. Apply the color to dry royal icing or fondant. Rinse your brush in a dish of water when switching between colors. The paint will dry within a few minutes.

PEARL DUST PAINT

This method is similar to painting with gel paste. Add a few drops of alcohol to the pearl dust to form an edible paint and apply it to the cookie. When painting with gold pearl dust, it's best to start with a brown icing base so that the gold stands out.

CRACKED GLAZE

This is a technique that I discovered by mistake. I'd iced a tray of cookies and accidentally stuck my finger into the icing after it started to crust over. The cracked surface of the icing reminded me of a piece of antique glazed pottery. I tried to replicate this effect using the same method (this time on purpose), but I couldn't seem to get it right. After a few icing experiments, I came up with this technique!

YOU'LL NEED

Completely dry white iced cookie (see p. 17 for instructions)

Scribe tool

Dark shade of matte dust, such as Wilton® Brown Color Dust

Round brush

Dry paper towel

1. Scratch the surface of the cookie's icing with a scribe tool to create "cracks."

2. Dust the surface with matte dust using a stippling motion with the brush. (Using a stippling motion helps to push the dust into the cracks.) Make sure to not touch the surface of the cookie before applying the dust. Otherwise, you might end up with visible fingerprints!

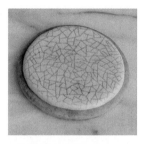

3. Wipe the brush on a dry paper towel to clean it before brushing the excess dust off the cookie.

QUICK TIP

Sometimes a toothpick is a suitable substitute for a scribe tool, but in this case, it's not— you'll need something that is very sturdy and sharp to make deep scratches in the surface of the icing.

Texture

This stippling technique can be used to create a furry look; it can also be used to make a sandy texture on a beach-y design.

1. Apply a small amount of flood consistency icing with a pastry bag fitted with a number 2 tip.

2. Using the brush, immediately dab the icing continuously until you have the desired amount of texture on the icing.

3. Repeat steps 1 and 2 until you've covered the desired area.

YOU'LL NEED

Completely dry iced cookie (see p. 17 for instructions)

12-inch pastry bag fitted with a number 2 piping tip and filled with flood consistency royal icing

Round brush

QUICK TIP

Work in small sections at a time so that the icing doesn't dry before you have a chance to stipple it with the brush.

BASKET WEAVE

This technique takes some patience, but the result is worth the effort! A basket weave pattern is perfect for a springtime cookie design.

YOU'LL NEED

12-inch pastry bag fitted with a number 3 piping tip and filled with stiff consistency royal icing

Completely dry iced cookie (see p. 17 for instructions)

1. Pipe a vertical line across the cookie with stiff consistency icing and a number 3 tip. Cover the line with short horizontal lines, leaving enough space in between each one so that the tip can fit between them. Pipe another vertical line.

2. Make the next set of horizontal lines by tucking the tip into the spaces between the lines so that it gives the illusion that the icing is coming up from underneath the first vertical line.

3. Continue this pattern until you've covered the desired area.

DRY DUSTING

Add a little shimmer to your cookies by brushing on some pearl dust.

1. Using the flat angled brush, apply dry pearl dust to the edges of a cookie by dipping the brush in the dust, placing the brush on the edge of the cookie, and flicking it in toward the center. You can also apply the dust in the seams of a quilted cookie to add dimension and shine.

YOU'LL NEED

Flat angled brush

Pearl dust

Completely dry iced cookie (see p. 17 for instructions)

QUICK TIP
It's best to use a flat angled brush rather than a soft round brush for this technique so that the dust only goes where you want it to and doesn't end up on the entire surface of the cookie.

COOKIE POPS

This method makes it easy to make any cookie into a cookie pop. When baking cookie pops, make sure that you're using cookie sticks that are meant to go into the oven.

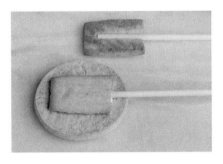

YOU'LL NEED

12 oven-safe cookie sticks

12 scrap rectangles of raw cookie dough, about 1½ inches wide by 2 inches tall

12-inch pastry bag fitted with a number 3 piping tip and filled with slightly thinned stiff consistency royal icing

12 decorated cookies

1. Press a cookie stick into a scrap of raw dough. Make sure to not press too hard—you don't want to make a hole in the dough. Transfer the cookie, stick side down, to a parchment-lined baking sheet.

2. Position a rack in the center of the oven and heat the oven to 350°F. Bake the cookie sticks, stick side down, 6 to 7 minutes, or until the edges are golden brown. Transfer to a rack to cool.

3. Once the cookie sticks are completely cool, use icing that is a little bit thinner than stiff consistency to attach it to the back of a completely dry decorated cookie with the stick side facing in.

4. Let the cookie pops dry flat on a baking sheet for about 4 hours.

QUICK TIP

This technique is a great way to make use of leftover cookie dough! Save your scraps in the freezer so that you'll have them on hand when you're ready to bake some cookie pops.

BUILDING A COOKIE BOX

What better way to wrap a gift than with an edible box? The measurements given here are just a suggestion; you can make your box as big or small as you'd like.

YOU'LL NEED

Template (see p. 136)

Paring knife

Sheet of well-chilled cookie dough (see p. 118, p. 120 or p. 122)

Small round cutter, approximately 1 inch

12-inch pastry decorating bags

Number 3 piping tip

Flood consistency royal icing

Stiff consistency icing, thinned slightly

Bag ties

QUICK TIP

The icing that holds the box pieces together should be somewhere between stiff and medium consistency. If it's too stiff, it'll flake off the cookie when it dries. If it's too thin, it will be difficult for the pieces to stick together.

1. Using the templates on p.136, cut the shapes from a chilled sheet of cookie dough. Use a small round cutter to make the handle of the lid. If you're using your own measurements to make a box, keep in mind that it will be easier to assemble if the sides are shorter than they are long so they won't flop over as easily after being glued together.

2. Bake and cool the cookie box pieces according to the recipe. If necessary, use a citrus zester to file the edges so that they're straight.

3. Fit a pastry bag with a number 3 piping tip and fill the bag with flood consistency royal icing. Ice the cookie box pieces and let them dry completely, about 8 hours. You can add decorations at this point, such as brush embroidery or molded fondant. Borders will be added later, after the box is assembled.

4. Fit a pastry bag with a number 3 piping tip and fill the bag with the slightly thinned stiff consistency royal icing. Place the bottom cookie box piece flat on your work surface. Pipe some of the icing on opposite sides of the bottom piece and attach both of the square side pieces. Hold the pieces together for about 30 seconds to make sure they stick.

5. Once the square sides are in place, apply icing to the rectangle side pieces and hold all of the sides together for about 30 seconds to make sure they adhere. If there are gaps in the corners of the box, pipe a border with a large tip to cover them later.

6. To assemble the lid, attach the smaller piece of the lid to the underside of the larger piece. This smaller piece will keep the lid from moving around once you place it on top of the box. Attach the handle to the top with a dab of icing. Allow the icing to dry for about 2 hours before adding borders and then let dry completely before handling the box, another 2 hours. Cut 4 small circles and attach them to the bottom of the box if you want to add feet.

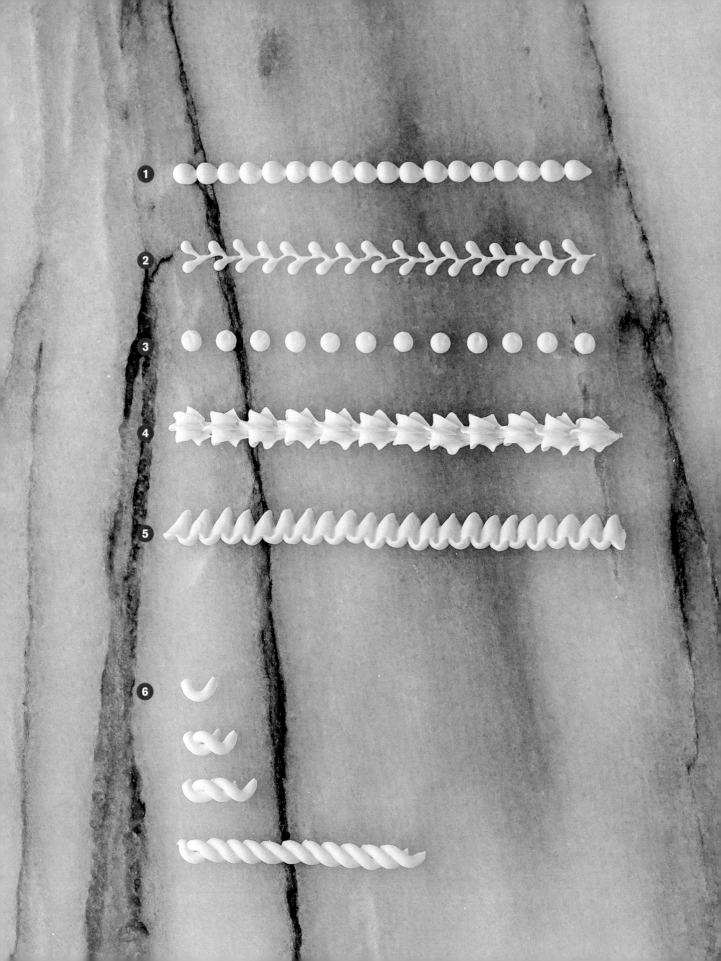

Borders & Trim

Now that you know several different cookie decorating techniques, you can add a finishing touch to your designs with some pretty borders and trim.

1. Bead Fit a pastry bag with a number 3 piping tip and fill the bag with stiff consistency royal icing. Holding the tip at a 45 degree angle slightly above the surface of the cookie, squeeze the bag and let the icing build up into a ball.

Stop squeezing and pull the tip away, making sure to bring the tip down and touch it to the cookie's surface to end the bead.

Start the next bead close enough to the first one so that it covers the end of it, but far enough away that the beads are not squished together.

2. Double Bead Fit a pastry bag with a number 1 piping tip and fill the bag with medium consistency royal icing. Holding the tip at a 45 degree angle slightly above the cookie's surface, squeeze the bag and let the icing build up into a ball.

Stop squeezing and drag the icing on the cookie's surface to create a small tail.

Pipe the next bead so that it forms a "Y" shape with the previous bead. Continue this pattern until you've covered the desired area.

3. Dots Fit a pastry bag with a number 3 piping tip and fill the bag with stiff consistency royal icing. Holding the tip at a 90 degree angle slightly above the cookie's surface, squeeze the bag and let the icing build up into a ball.

Stop squeezing and move the tip around the edge of the bead counterclockwise to create a smooth surface on the dot. If you pull straight up without moving the tip around, you'll end up with a peak.

4. Shell Fit a pastry bag with a number 18 star tip and fill the bag with stiff consistency royal icing. Holding the tip at a 45 degree angle slightly above the surface of the cookie, squeeze the bag and let the icing build up into a shell. While squeezing, move the tip very slightly forward to help widen it at the top.

Stop squeezing and pull the tip away, making sure to bring the tip down to touch the cookie's surface to end the shell.

5. Ruffle Fit a pastry bag with a number 101 petal piping tip and fill the bag with stiff consistency royal icing.

Holding the tip with the wide end on the cookie's surface and the narrow end facing up at a 45 degree angle, squeeze the bag and move the tip in a zigzag motion to create a ruffled edge, keeping the wide end of the tip touching the surface.

6. Rope Fit a pastry bag with a number 3 piping tip and fill the bag with stiff consistency royal icing. Start out by piping a "U" shape.

Tuck the tip into the curve of the U and pipe a backward "S" shape. While piping the S, make sure to lift the tip up off the surface so that the icing is not lying flat. This will give your rope a nice round shape.

Next, tuck the tip into the second curve of the backward S and pipe another backward S, keeping the curves tight so as not to create gaps between them. Continue this motion to create a rope.

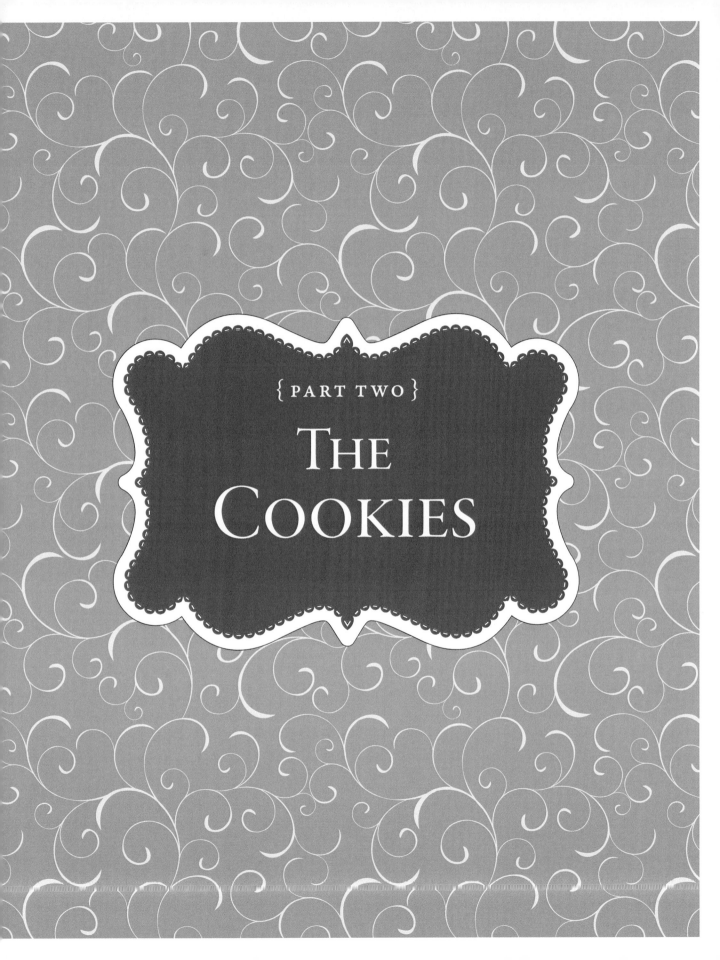

{ PART TWO }

THE COOKIES

{2}

FLOWERS & FILIGREE

SPRINGTIME IS WHEN I'M MOST INSPIRED TO DECORATE WITH FLOWERS and filigree—the world is coming back to life with so many pretty colors popping up out of the ground. This time of year also brings Easter and Mother's Day, which are both perfect reasons to celebrate with cookies. But you don't have to wait for spring to make the designs in this chapter—anyone would be happy to receive these edible works of art year-round.

Hyacinth Cookie Pops

These colorful cookie pops would make a beautiful centerpiece for a Sunday brunch. Make the 5-petal flowers ahead of time by piping them out on a piece of wax paper. Allow them to dry completely and store them in an airtight container until you're ready to decorate. Attach them to the cookie with a dab of icing.

YOU'LL NEED

Hyacinth flower and leaf template (you'll need two or three leaves for each flower, see p. 135)

Egg-shape cookie cutter

Cookie dough (see p. 118, p. 120 or p. 122)

Oven-safe cookie sticks

12-inch pastry bag fitted with a number 81 piping tip and filled with white stiff consistency royal icing

12-inch pastry bag fitted with a number 2 piping tip and filled with green stiff consistency royal icing

12-inch pastry bag fitted with a number 3 piping tip and filled with dark green flood consistency royal icing

12-inch pastry bag fitted with a number 1 piping tip and filled with light green flood consistency royal icing

Scribe tool or toothpick

Floral tape (optional)

COLORS

Green = Wilton® Juniper Green

TO MAKE THE HYACINTH COOKIE POPS

1. Use an egg-shape cutter to cut the flower and the leaf cookies, then use the template on p. 135 to trim them. Bake and cool the cookies according to the recipe.

2. Cover the larger of the two cookies with 5-petal flowers: pipe one petal at a time with white stiff consistency icing using tip number 81, starting from the area that will be the flower center. Begin by touching the bottom of the curved tip to the cookie. Then squeeze and lift until the petal is about ½ inch long. Stop squeezing the bag before you pull the tip away. Repeat this motion for the rest of the petals. Pipe a dot of green stiff consistency icing in the center of each flower.

3. To make the leaves, ice the cookies with dark green flood consistency icing and number 3 tip. Immediately pipe veins with the lighter shade of green flood consistency icing and number 1 tip. Use the scribe tool to feather the veins out toward the edges of the cookie. Remember to work quickly so that the icing doesn't start to crust over before you feather the veins. Allow the flowers and leaves to dry completely, about 8 hours.

4. Attached the baked cookie sticks to the back of the decorated cookies according to the instructions on p.31. You can wrap the sticks in floral tape, if you like.

DRESS IT UP!

Display the cookie pops in a brightly colored flowerpot filled with granulated sugar to keep them upright.

Quilted Eggs

The shimmery quilted pattern on these cookies was inspired by Fabergé. My grandmother sold Fabergé eggs in her store, along with so many other beautiful things that have inspired my work throughout the years.

YOU'LL NEED

Un-iced 4-inch egg-shape cookies

12-inch pastry bag fitted with a number 2 piping tip and filled with green flood consistency royal icing

Flat angled brush

Dark shade of gold pearl dust, such as Wilton® Bronze or Crystal Colors® Chocolate Gold

12-inch pastry bag fitted with a number 3 piping tip and filled with white stiff consistency royal icing

Completely dry piped rose (see p. 24)

12-inch pastry bag fitted with a number 352 piping tip and filled with green stiff consistency royal icing

White pearl dust

Round brush

Alcohol or flavored extract

Palette or small dish

Eyedropper

COLORS

Green = Wilton® Juniper Green

Blue = Wilton® Delphinium Blue

TO MAKE THE QUILTED EGGS

1. Ice the cookies with green flood consistency icing using the quilting technique shown on p. 20. Let the icing dry completely, about 8 hours.

2. With a flat angled brush, apply a dark shade of pearl dust in the seams of the quilt.

3. Pipe dots with white stiff consistency icing at each intersection of the tufts, as described on p. 35. Apply the piped rose in the center.

4. Add leaves with green stiff consistency icing according to the instructions on p. 24.

5. Use the eyedropper to mix a few drops of alochol or flavored extract with white pearl dust in a palette and paint the dots with a round brush according to the instructions on p. 27.

Piped Rose Eggs

The pretty pink piped roses on these cookies were inspired by the porcelain roses on a set of my favorite lamps, given to me by my aunt. Try experimenting with different tip sizes and shapes for a variation on this design; a number 59s, for example, will give you a beautiful tiny rose with curved petals.

DESIGNS

YOU'LL NEED

12-inch pastry bag fitted with a number 3 piping tip and filled with blue flood consistency royal icing

Un-iced 4-inch egg-shape cookies

Completely dry piped roses (you'll need between 7 and 10 roses per cookie, see p. 24)

12-inch pastry bag fitted with a number 352 piping tip and filled with green stiff consistency royal icing

12-inch pastry bag fitted with a number 3 piping tip and filled with white stiff consistency royal icing

COLORS

Blue = Wilton® Delphinium Blue

Pink = Wilton® Aster Mauve

Green = Wilton® Juniper Green

TO MAKE THE PIPED ROSE EGGS

1. Ice the cookies with blue flood consistency icing according to the instructions on p. 17 and let dry completely, about 8 hours.

2. Arrange the piped roses on the cookie. Once you're happy with the design, attach the roses with green stiff consistency icing. Add leaves with the green icing according to the instructions on p. 24.

3. Pipe a bead border with the white icing as described on p. 35.

DRESS IT UP!

Paint the beads with white pearl dust for a shimmery border. See p. 27 for instructions.

Flower Baskets

The basket weave technique is a classic in cake decorating, but it's equally gorgeous on cookies. You can add flowers to these baskets as shown here, or get creative and add some eggs or bunny ears.

YOU'LL NEED

Un-iced 3-inch round cookies

12-inch decorating bag fitted with a number 3 piping tip and filled with blue flood consistency royal icing

Scribe tool

12-inch pastry bag fitted with a number 3 piping tip and filled with white stiff consistency royal icing

12-inch pastry bag fitted with a number 352 piping tip and filled with green stiff consistency royal icing

12-inch pastry bag fitted with a number 2 piping tip and filled with pink stiff consistency royal icing

COLORS

Blue = Wilton® Delphinium Blue

Green = Wilton® Juniper Green

Pink = Wilton® Aster Mauve

TO MAKE THE FLOWER BASKETS

1. Ice the cookies with blue flood consistency icing according to the instructions on p. 17 and let dry completely, about 8 hours.

2. Using a scribe tool, draw a slightly curved line across the center of the cookie as a guide for the top of the basket.

3. Pipe a basket with white stiff consistency icing using the basket weave technique shown on p. 30.

4. Add a rope border for the handle with white stiff consistency icing following the instructions on p. 35.

5. Pipe teardrop shapes with pink stiff consistency icing to create little flowers. Add leaves with green stiff consistency icing as described on p. 24. Finish the design with a few more pink dots on the leaves.

Gold Filigree

The filigree design is one that I've been doodling on paper for as long as I can remember—I filled plenty of notebooks with it during my days at school! You can use the template on p. 134 to practice your filigree piping skills, or use it along with the tissue paper method shown on p. 21 to trace the design directly onto the cookie.

YOU'LL NEED

Un-iced 3-inch round cookies

12-inch pastry bags fitted with number 3 piping tips and filled with blue, pink, green, and light brown flood consistency royal icing

Filigree template (p. 134)

12-inch pastry bag fitted with a number 2 piping tip and filled with light brown medium consistency royal icing

Gold pearl dust, such as Crystal Colors@ Antique Gold

Alcohol or flavored extract

Palette or small dish

Eyedropper

Round brush

COLORS

Blue = Wilton® Delphinium Blue

Pink = Wilton® Aster Mauve

Green = Wilton® Juniper Green

Light brown = AmeriColor® Chocolate Brown + a touch of Wilton® Juniper Green

TO MAKE THE GOLD FILIGREE

1. Ice the cookies with different color flood consistency icings according to the instructions on p. 17 and let them dry completely, about 8 hours.

2. Pipe a filigree design with light brown medium consistency icing onto each cookie.

3. Add dots around the border with the light brown icing according to the instructions on p. 35 and let the icing dry about 30 minutes.

4. Use the eyedropper to mix a few drops of alochol or flavored extract with gold pearl dust in a palette and paint the filigree with a round brush according to the instructions on p. 27.

TIPS FOR PIPING FILIGREE

When piping filigree, change the pressure on the pastry bag for varying thicknesses in the lines. Start with heavy pressure, allow the icing to build up, and then release the pressure as you move the tip to create the curves in this design.

Birds and Filigree

The adorable birds on these cookies were inspired by a set of salt and pepper shakers that belonged to my grandmother and were given to me by my mom. This design combines some of my favorite techniques: royal icing transfers, brush embroidery, and filigree.

YOU'LL NEED

12-inch pastry bag fitted with a number 2 piping tip and filled with white flood consistency royal icing

Bird template (p. 134)

Wax paper

Cake board, baking sheet, or other hard surface such as a Plexiglas® board

Masking tape

Scribe tool

12-inch pastry bag fitted with a number 3 piping tip and filled with white stiff consistency royal icing

Square tip brush

Dish of water

Dry paper towel

12-inch pastry bag fitted with a number 3 piping tip and filled with blue flood consistency royal icing

12-inch pastry bag fitted with a number 1 tip and filled with light brown flood consistency royal icing

Un-iced 2¼-inch square cookies

Filigree template (p. 134)

COLORS

Blue = Wilton® Delphinium Blue

Light brown = AmeriColor® Chocolate Brown + a touch of Wilton® Juniper Green

TO MAKE THE BIRDS AND FLIGREE

1. Place the bird template on a cake board, baking sheet or Plexiglass® board, cover with wax paper and secure with masking tape as described on p. 22. Pipe the birds with white flood consistency icing and use the scribe tool to drag the icing into the thin areas of the beak and the end of the tail.

2. Before removing the template from the wax paper, add a brush embroidered wing using white stiff consistency icing. Dip the square tip brush in a dish of water and blot it on the dry paper towel before brushing the icing as described on p. 23. The wing has 3 layers of brush embroidery; start on the lowest area of the wing and work your way up.

3. Ice a square cookie with blue flood consistency icing and a number 3 tip according to the instructions on p. 17, and immediately pipe a filigree design with light brown flood consistency icing and a number 1 tip. (See the filigree template on p. 134 to help you to practice). While the icing is still wet, apply the bird transfer, and let the icing dry completely, about 8 hours.

4. Using white stiff consistency icing and number 3 tip, add a dot border according to the instructions on p. 35

QUICK TIP

Make the bird transfers ahead of time, let them dry, and store them in an airtight container at room temperature until you're ready to decorate the cookies.

{3}

Treasures & Gifts

A BEAUTIFUL HANDMADE TREAT IS PERFECT FOR ANY OCCASION.

These sweets can be used as a dessert table centerpiece, or wrapped up as a gift for someone special. These stunning sweets will brighten anyone's day!

Ocean Cookies

The gold coral, fondant shells, and royal icing starfish on these pale sea foam green cookies take me back to summer vacation on Cape Cod. You don't have to wait for warm weather to make these beach-y cookies!

YOU'LL NEED

12-inch pastry bag fitted with a number 1 piping tip and filled with light brown medium consistency royal icing

Starfish template (see p. 134)

Wax paper

Cake board, baking sheet, or other hard surface such as a Plexiglas® board

Masking tape

Palette or small dish

Eyedropper

Round brush

Gold pearl dust, such as Crystal Colors™ Antique Gold

Alcohol or flavored extract

12-inch pastry bag fitted with a number 3 piping tip and filled with sea foam green flood consistency royal icing

Un-iced 2 ¼-inch square cookies

12-inch pastry bag fitted with a number 18 star piping tip and filled with white stiff consistency royal icing

1-inch ball of white fondant

½-inch ball of light brown fondant

Flexible shell mold (approximately 1½-inches)

Cornstarch

12-inch pastry bag fitted with a number 4 piping tip and filled with white stiff consistency royal icing

TO MAKE THE STARFISH

1. Place the starfish template on a cake board, baking sheet or Plexiglass® board, cover with wax paper and secure with masking tape as described on p. 22. Pipe the starfish with medium consistency brown icing and a tip nunber 1. Once dry, add small dots with the brown icing along each point of the starfish.

2. While the starfish are still on the wax paper, Use the eyedropper to mix a few drops of alochol or flavored extract with gold pearl dust in a palette and paint them with a round brush according to the instructions on p. 27. Once the gold paint is dry, you can peel the starfish from the wax paper.

3. Ice a square cookie with sea foam green flood consistency icing as shown on p. 17, place a starfish transfer on the cookie, and let the icing dry completely, about 8 hours.

4. Add individual shells with white stiff consistency icing and a number 18 tip around the edge as described on p. 35.

TO MAKE THE SHELL

1. Roll the white and brown fondant into logs and twist them together to create a marbled effect. Don't overmix the colors; they shouldn't blend together completely. Once you have the desired amount of marbling, dust the shell mold with cornstarch and press the fondant into the mold. (Refer to the instructions on p. 25 for more about using flexible molds.)

2. Ice the cookie with the sea foam green icing, place the shell on the cookie, and let the icing dry completely, about 8 hours.

3. Add a dot of white stiff consistency icing with a number 4 tip on each corner.

COLORS

Sea foam green = Wilton®
Delphinium Blue + a touch of
Wilton® Juniper Green

Brown = AmeriColor® Chocolate
Brown

DRESS IT UP!

Paint the shells and dots
with white pearl dust ac-
cording to the instructions
on p. 27 for even more
sparkle!

TO MAKE THE CORAL

1. Ice the cookie with the sea foam green icing and let dry
completely, about 8 hours.

2. Pipe a branchy coral design with brown medium consistency
icing and let it dry about 1 hour.

3. Paint the coral with gold pearl dust according to the
instructions on p. 27.

4. Add a dot with white stiff consistency icing and a number 4
tip on each corner.

Cookie Box

A cookie box is a beautiful and creative way to wrap an edible gift. This design was inspired by a set of early nineteenth century French mirrors that I found in an antique shop during a family vacation to Sandwich, Massachusetts.

YOU'LL NEED

Baked box pieces, cut from the box template on p. 136

12-inch pastry bag fitted with a number 3 piping tip and filled with light blue flood consistency royal icing

4 oz. white fondant

Cornstarch

Flexible molds

12-inch pastry bag fitted with a number 3 tip and filled with slightly thinned white stiff consistency royal icing

12-inch pastry bag fitted with a number 18 piping tip and filled with white stiff consistency royal icing

12-inch pastry bag fitted with a number 5 piping tip and filled with white stiff consistency royal icing

Completely dry mini cookies decorated with wet-on-wet roses (shown on p. 18) to fill the box, about 2 dozen

COLORS

Light blue = Wilton® Delphinium Blue + a touch of Juniper Green

Blue = Wilton® Delphinium Blue

Pink = Wilton® Aster Mauve

Green = Wilton® Juniper Green

TO MAKE THE COOKIE BOX

1. Ice the sides, the handle, and the larger of the two lid pieces of the box with the blue icing according to the instructions on p 17. Let dry completely, about 8 hours.

2. Mold fondant decorations according to the instructions on p. 25. Attach the decorations with a dab of light blue flood consistency icing.

3. Assemble the box according to the instructions on p. 32, using white slightly thinned flood consistency icing as glue to hold the pieces together. Let the icing dry about 2 hours.

4. Pipe a shell border in each corner with white stiff consistency icing and number 18 tip as described on p. 35.

5. Add a bead border with white stiff consistency icing and number 5 tip to the top and bottom edge and around the handle according to the instructions on p. 35.

6. Let the box dry completely, about 8 hours, before filling with mini cookies.

QUICK TIP

Remember, you can make your own flexible molds using food-safe mold-making material, or buy pre-made molds online.

Fondant Rose Petals

Adorned with delicate rose petals surrounded by a string of pearls, these cookies are sure to impress. To get a head start, Make the rose petals up to a week in advance, store them in an airtight container and apply them to the cookie when you're ready to decorate!

YOU'LL NEED

3x3-inch square cookie

12-inch pastry bag fitted with a number 3 piping tip and filled with white flood consistency royal icing

Fondant rose petals from p. 26 (You will need 3 rose petals per cookie.)

12-inch pastry bag fitted with a number 5 piping tip and filled with white stiff consistency royal icing

White pearl dust

Palette or small dish

Eyedropper

Alcohol or flavored extract

Round brush

QUICK TIP

You can also use these fondant rose petals to decorate other desserts, like the brownies shown on p. 115.

TO MAKE THE FONDANT ROSE PETALS

1. Ice a cookie with white flood consistency icing according to the instructions on p. 17 and let dry completely, about 8 hours.

2. Form and color 3 fondant rose petals for each cookie according to the instructions on p. 26. Brush the back of the petals with a bit of white flood consistency icing and attach them to the cookie.

3. Add pearls with white stiff consistency royal icing using the bead border method described on p. 35. Let the beads dry about 30 minutes.

4. Use an eyedropper to add a few drops of alcohol or flavored extract to white pearl dust in a palette. Paint the beads with a round brush according to the instructions on p. 27.

Hand-Painted Roses

When I was growing up, visiting my grandparents at their home in New Jersey was one of my favorite things to do. These hand-painted rose cookies were inspired by their kitchen cabinets; each was embellished with a gold rimmed knob with a tiny rose in the center.

YOU'LL NEED

12-inch pastry bag fitted with a number 3 piping tip and filled with white flood consistency royal icing

Palette or small dishes

Pink gel paste

Green gel paste

Dry paper towel

One dozen 1½-inch cookies

Round brush

Fine tip brush

Gold pearl dust, such as Crystal Colors™ Antique Gold

Alcohol or flavored extract

Eyedropper

Paint palette or small dish

COLORS

Pink = Wilton® Aster Mauve

Green = Wilton® Juniper Green

QUICK TIP

If you make a mistake, wash away the paint with a damp brush and then blot the spot with a dry paper towel.

TO MAKE THE HAND PAINTED ROSES

1. Ice the cookie with white flood consistency icing as shown on p. 17 and let dry completely, about 8 hours.

2. You'll need two shades of pink and two shades of green for this design. To make a light shade of pink, place a tiny dot of pink gel paste food coloring onto palette and add a few drops of alcohol or flavored extract using the eyedropper as described on p. 27. For the darker shade, place a pea-size amount of gel paste food coloring into a separate dish and add one drop of liquid for a thicker consistency. Repeat this process with green gel paste to make two shades of green edible paint.

3. Use a round brush to paint an oval slightly above the center of the cookie using the light shade of pink. Allow the paint to dry 1 to 2 minutes. Then, using the fine tip brush, apply the darker shade in short, curved strokes, starting in the center and working out toward the edges. These strokes, which represent the rose petals, should be short and tight in the center, and more separated and longer as you work your way out toward the edges.

4. To make the leaves, use the round brush to paint two leaves with the light shade of green. Let dry 1 to 2 minutes, and then, using the fine tip brush, paint a vein with the darker shade, starting at the base of the rose and moving the brush toward the end of the leaf for a tapered line.

5. Use the fine tip brush to paint an outline with a mixture of gold pearl dust and alcohol as described on p. 27. If you're not comfortable painting the gold outline freehand, make a guide on the cookie by tracing a small round cookie cutter with an edible ink marker.

Marbled Cookies

Marbling is a simple technique with an impressive result. This design has a contemporary vibe, but adding a fondant rose in a dusty shade of pink gives it a more vintage feel.

YOU'LL NEED

3x3-inch square cookies

12-inch pastry bags fitted with number 3 piping tips and filled with white, blue, and green flood consistency royal icing

Scribe tool

12-inch pastry bag fitted with a number 1 piping tip and filled with white medium consistency royal icing

Rose mold (I made mine with food-safe mold making material and a plastic rose bead from the craft store)

Cornstarch, for dusting the mold

1-inch ball deep rose colored fondant for each flower

COLORS

Blue: Wilton® Delphinium Blue

Green: Wilton® Juniper Green

Deep rose: Wilton® Aster Mauve + a touch of AmeriColor® Chocolate Brown

TO MAKE THE MARBLED COOKIES

1. Ice the cookie with the white flood consistency icing, and then immediately pipe alternating stripes of blue and green. Drag the scribe tool up and down through the icing as shown on p. 19. Allow the icing to dry completely.

2. Pipe a double bead border with the white medium consistency icing according to the instructions on p. 35.

3. Fill a rose mold dusted with cornstarch with rose colored fondant. Make sure to press the fondant into the mold enough so that all of the crevices are filled. Remove the fondant from the mold as shown on p. 25. Attach the fondant to the cookie with a dab of medium consistency icing.

QUICK TIP

If you'll be packaging the cookies, make the fondant roses ahead and let them dry overnight before attaching them to the cookies. This will lessen the chance that they'll get damaged.

Jewelry Cookies

Dress up your cookies with royal icing chains and fondant charms, and then make them shine with gold and white pearl dust. Half the fun of making these cookies is finding pretty little buttons and beads to create the molds, so take a look around your house or in the craft store to find unique pieces.

YOU'LL NEED

Cornstarch, for dusting

Assorted jewelry charm molds (I made my molds with food-safe mold making material and some buttons)

½-inch ball brown fondant for each charm

¼-inch ball of white fondant for each charm (optional)

12-inch pastry bag fitted with a number 3 piping tip and filled with blue flood consistency royal icing

3x3-inch square cookies

Scribe tool

12-inch pastry bag fitted with a number 1 piping tip and filled with brown medium consistency royal icing

Bronze pearl dust

Alcohol or flavored extract

Eyedropper

White pearl dust (optional)

Round brush

Palette or small dish for mixing the pearl dust

COLORS

Blue: Wilton® Delphinium Blue

Brown: AmeriColor® Chocolate Brown + a touch of Juniper Green

TO MAKE THE JEWELRY COOKIES

1. Dust a jewelry mold with cornstarch, and fill the mold with brown fondant, pressing down so that all of the crevices are filled. Remove the fondant from the mold as shown on p. 25. If your mold has a place for a "stone," fill that area first with white fondant and then press the brown fondant on top.

2. Ice a square cookie with the blue flood consistency icing and number 3 tip according to the instructions on p. 17. Let the icing dry completely, about 8 hours. Use a scribe tool to scratch an outline of where you want the chains to hang on the cookie. You can make one chain or a few, but be sure to leave enough room for the charms.

3. Follow the instructions on p. 35 for piping a bead border with the brown medium consistency icing to create chains over the lines. Attach the fondant charm to the cookie using a dab of brown icing. Make a "jump ring" at the top of each charm by piping a small loop over the chain. Allow the icing to dry about 30 minutes.

4. Use an eyedropper to add a few drops of alcohol or flavored extract to bronze pearl dust to form a paint according to the instructions on p. 27. Use a soft round brush to paint the charms and the chains. If your charms contain white fondant, paint those areas with white pearl dust.

QUICK TIP

The fondant jewelry can be molded and painted ahead of time. Let it dry overnight to save it for later use.

{4}

AUTUMN TREATS

WHEN THE LEAVES BEGIN TO CHANGE, IT'S TIME TO CELEBRATE

the new season with some sweet treats. In this chapter, you'll

find inspiration for delicious designs that are perfect for fall.

Watercolor Leaves

You don't need icing to make these realistic-looking fall leaves; just apply edible watercolor paints directly to the bare surface of the cookie.

YOU'LL NEED

Alcohol or flavored extract

Eyedropper

Green gel paste food coloring

Red gel paste food coloring

Yellow gel paste food coloring

Paint palette or small dish

Round brush

Un-iced 3-inch leaf-shaped cookies

Dry paper towel

COLORS

Brown = AmeriColor® Chocolate Brown

Red = AmeriColor® Tulip Red

Yellow = Wilton® Buttercup Yellow

Green = Wilton® Juniper Green

TO MAKE THE WATERCOLOR LEAVES

1. Add a few drops of alcohol or flavored extract using an eyedropper to gel paste food colorings in a paint palette or small dish as shown on p. 27 to create edible watercolor paints.

2. Before applying color to the cookie, test the paint on a dry paper towel to make sure the color as is desired. Use a soft round brush to apply large splotches of green, yellow, and red to the bare cookie, rinsing your brush well between colors.

3. Paint a brown vein up the center of the leaf. Paint smaller veins branching out from the center toward the edges.

PAINTING TIPS

Don't be afraid to get creative with the colors and patterns on these cookies! The more variations there are in the cookies, the more natural they'll look. Try making the veins in the leaves gold instead of brown, using a mixture of gold pearl dust and alcohol or flavored extract.

Marbled Leaves

Here's a different take on the fall leaf cookie. This design uses the marbling technique to blend the colors together.

YOU'LL NEED

Un-iced 5-inch leaf-shape cookies

12-inch pastry bags fitted with number 3 piping tips and filled with light brown, burgundy, auburn, yellow, and green flood consistency royal icing

Scribe tool

12-inch pastry bag fitted with a number 1 piping tip and filled with dark brown flood consistency royal icing

COLORS

Light and dark brown = AmeriColor® Chocolate Brown + a touch of Juniper Green

Burgundy = AmeriColor® Tulip Red + a touch of AmeriColor® Chocolate Brown + a touch of AmeriColor® Tulip Red

Auburn = AmeriColor® Chocolate Brown + a touch of AmeriColor® Tulip Red

Yellow = Wilton® Buttercup Yellow

Green = Wilton® Juniper Green

TO MAKE THE MARBLED LEAVES

1. Ice the cookie with sections of green, yellow, burgundy, light brown and auburn flood consistency icing.

2. Using the scribe tool, marble the colors together. Remember that you'll have about 5 minutes to marble the icing before it starts to crust over.

3. While the iced cookie is still wet, pipe a vein of dark brown icing down the center and smaller veins out toward the edges of the cookie.

4. Drag the scribe tool down the center of each vein, feathering the edges to make even smaller veins throughout the leaf for a more natural look.

Quilted Pumpkins

As I was walking through a pumpkin patch on a Hudson Valley farm, I spotted a white pumpkin in a sea of orange and brown. As I got closer, I saw that it wasn't actually white, but a very pale shade of greenish blue, which immediately inspired me to create this design. These cookies are made using a similar technique to that of the quilted cookie shown on p. 20.

YOU'LL NEED

Edible ink marker in any color

Un-iced pumpkin-shape cookies

12-inch pastry bag fitted with a number 2 piping tip and filled with pale blue-green flood consistency royal icing

Gold pearl dust, such as Crystal Colors™ Antique Gold or Wilton® Gold

Flat angled brush

12-inch pastry bag fitted with a number 2 piping tip and filled with green stiff consistency icing

12-inch pastry bag fitted with a number 352 leaf piping tip and filled with green stiff consistency royal icing

COLORS

Pale blue-green = Wilton® Delphinium Blue + Juniper Green

Green = Wilton® Juniper Green

TO MAKE THE QUILTED PUMPKINS

1. Using an edible ink marker, draw lines to divide the cookie into 5 or 7 sections.

2. Fill in every other section with pale blue-green flood consistency icing and number 2 tip. Let the icing dry at least 1 hour.

3. Fill in the remaining sections and let the icing dry completely, about 8 hours.

4. Apply gold pearl dust between each section with a flat angled brush to add definition and shine.

5. Pipe a vine and cover the stem with vertical lines using green stiff consistency icing and number 2 tip.

6. With green stiff consistency icing and number 352 leaf piping tip, add leaves to the vine.

Skull Cameos

*Fondant cameos are one of my favorite ways to dress up a cookie.
These fondant skulls are a creepy, twist on the original and will make
your cookies hauntingly beautiful!*

YOU'LL NEED

12-inch pastry bag fitted with a number 3 piping tip and filled with taupe flood consistency royal icing

½-inch ball of white fondant

½-inch ball of dark gray fondant

Skull cameo flexible mold (you'll find skull cameo molds online at Etsy.com)

Scribe tool

Rose bud flexible mold (I made my own with food-safe mold making material)

Cornstarch for dusting the mold

Un-iced 2¼-inch-square cookies

12-inch pastry bag fitted with a number 2 piping tip and filled with dark gray medium consistency royal icing

Flat angled brush

Bronze pearl, such as Wilton® Bronze

Gold pearl dust, such as Crystal Colors™ Antique Gold

COLORS

Taupe = AmeriColor® Chocolate Brown + a touch of AmeriColor® Super Black

Dark Gray = AmeriColor® Super Black

TO MAKE THE SKULL CAMEOS

1. Ice the cookie with the taupe icing as described on p. 17 and let dry completely, about 8 hours.

2. To make the cameo, dust the skull mold with cornstarch, and press white fondant into the details of the skull mold; use the scribe tool to help push the icing into the tiny crevices. Fill the rest of the mold with dark gray fondant and press down to make sure the mold is completely filled. Remove the cameo from the mold. Use the same process to make the dark gray roses, using one color of fondant instead of two. See p. 25 for more on using fondant molds.

3. Attach the cameo and the roses to the cookie with a dab of medium consistency icing.

4. Pipe the scrolls under the cameo, the corner details, and the bead border with the gray medium consistency icing. See p. 35 for instructions on piping a bead border.

5. For an antiqued effect, use a flat angled brush to dust the edges of the cookies with bronze pearl dust. Lightly brush the cameos and the roses with gold pearl dust.

QUICK TIP

Make the fondant decorations ahead of time and save them until you're ready to decorate the cookies.

{5}

FROSTY SWEETS

WHEN THE WEATHER TURNS CHILLY, IT'S TIME TO HEAT UP THE oven and bake festive decorated cookies to share with friends and family. Not only great treats for parties, these can also be wrapped in colorful boxes or vintage cookie tins for gift giving.

Place Card Cookies

Personalized party favors are always a welcome treat, so why not dress up your table with some edible place cards? Don't worry if you're not comfortable with piping script. You can use the Tissue Paper Method (see p. 21) to help make a guide for perfect piping.

DESIGNS

YOU'LL NEED

Raw cookie dough (see p. 118, p. 120 or p. 122)

Paring knife for cutting the cookies

Place card cookie template, p. 135

12-inch pastry bag fitted with a number 3 piping tip and filled with ivory flood consistency royal icing

Piece of tissue paper (big enough to cover the cookie)

Edible ink marker in any color

Name printed out on a piece of paper

12-inch pastry bag fitted with a number 1 piping tip and filled with brown medium consistency royal icing

12-inch pastry bag fitted with a number 2 piping tip and filled with green medium consistency royal icing

12-inch pastry bag fitted with a number 2 piping tip and filled with red stiff consistency royal icing

Gold pearl dust, such as Crystal Colors™ Blush Gold

Round brush

Alcohol or flavored extract

Eyedropper

Paint palette or small dish

COLORS

Ivory: A touch of AmeriColor® Chocolate Brown, plus a touch of Wilton® Juniper Green

Brown: AmeriColor® Chocolate Brown, plus a touch of Wilton® Juniper Green

TO MAKE THE PLACE CARD COOKIES

1. Use the template from p. 135 to cut out the place card cookies and stands. Bake and cool the cookies according to the recipe.

2. Ice the place card cookie completely with the ivory flood consistency icing as described on p. 17. Let the icing dry completely, about 8 hours.

3. With the tissue paper, the edible ink marker, and the printed name, use the Tissue Paper Method shown on p. 21 to transfer the name onto the cookie. (You can pipe the name freehand rather than using the tissue paper method if you're more comfortable doing that.) Pipe over the name with the brown medium consistency icing, and then use the same icing and tip to pipe the fleur-de-lis design on either side of the name.

4. Pipe a garland with the green medium consistency icing. Add berries with the red icing using the dot method on p. 35. Let the icing dry about 30 minutes

5. Add a few drops of alcohol or flavored extract to gold pearl dust with the eyedropper as described on p. 27 and paint over the lettering.

6. Attach the stand to the back of the place card cookie using brown medium consistency icing. Hold the pieces together for about 30 seconds to make sure they stick.

Snowflakes

Just like real snowflakes, each one of these gingerbread cookies is a little bit different. Use your imagination to create a variety of shapes. A simple pattern can make for a dazzling design with the addition of a little bit of sparkling sugar!

YOU'LL NEED

Un-iced snowflake-shape cookies

12-inch pastry bags fitted with number 3 piping tips and filled with white and blue flood consistency royal icing

Scribe tool

White sparkling or sanding sugar

A piece of parchment or wax paper to catch the sparkling sugar

COLOR

Blue: Wilton® Delphinium Blue

TO MAKE THE SNOWFLAKES

1. Ice a snowflake cookie one point at a time with white or blue icing as described on p. 17. Use the scribe tool to pull the icing out to the edges and make the points on the snowflake nice and sharp.

2. Immediately place the cookie on the parchment or wax paper and cover the cookie with a generous amount of sparkling sugar. Remove the excess sugar by turning the cookie on its side and shaking gently.

3. When you're finished, fold the piece of paper and use it to help pour the sugar back into the container.

Ornaments

My grandmother's hand-sewn ornaments were the inspiration for these festive cookies. The tiny icing "stitches" take some patience to pipe, but the end result is worth the effort.

YOU'LL NEED

Raw cookie dough (See p. 118. p. 120 or p. 122)

8-point star cookie cutter

3-inch round cookie cutter

Decorating tip number 8 for cutting a small hole in the cookies

Edible ink marker in any color

12-inch pastry bags fitted with number 3 piping tips and filled with white and red flood consistency icing

12-inch pastry bags fitted with number 1 piping tips and filled with white and red medium consistency icing

Scribe tool

String or ribbon

COLORS

Red: AmeriColor® Tulip Red + a touch of Chocolate Brown + a touch of Black

IMPROVISE

If you don't have an 8-pointed star cookie cutter, you can cut the cookies using a 3x3-inch square template. Cut around the 4 corners of the square, then rotate it 90 degrees and cut around the 4 corners again.

TO MAKE THE ORNAMENTS

1. Cut the cookies into the desired shapes. Before baking the cookies, use a number 8 piping tip to cut a small hole in the top of each one. Bake the cookies according to the instructions.

2. Use an edible ink marker to divide the star cookie into 8 equal sections. Ice every other section of the cookie with white flood consistency icing and a number 3 tip. Let the icing dry about 1 hour. Then, fill in the remaining sections with red flood consistency icing.

3. Ice the round cookie with red flood consistency icing and a number 3 tip according to the instructions on p. 17. Allow the icing to dry completely, about 8 hours.

4. Using medium consistency icing and a number 1 tip, pipe red stitches on the white sections of the star cookie and white stitches on the red sections. The stitches are made up of tiny lines of icing, about 1/4 inch long.

5. To make the tree on the round cookie, use the scribe tool to scratch the outline of a triangle into the icing. Then, scratch horizontal lines across the triangle about 1/4 inch apart. Don't forget the tree trunk!

6. Pipe over the lines with white medium consistency icing and a number 1 tip. Fill in the spaces between the lines with small dots to complete the pattern.

7. Make a border of stitches on the round cookie using white medium consistency icing, just like on the star cookie. Allow the details to dry about an hour.

8. Tie a piece of string or ribbon through the hole. Now your edible ornaments are ready to decorate the tree!

Snow Globes

These adorable cookies are brought to life with a sprinkling of white nonpareils. Use the edible stands to prop them up, or lay them flat to arrange on a platter. Either way, these wintery scenes make fun and festive treats!

YOU'LL NEED

Raw cookie dough (see p. 118. p. 120 or p. 122

Snow globe template from p. 137

Paring knife to cut the cookies

12-inch pastry bags fitted with number 3 piping tips and filled with blue, white, and red flood consistency icing

12-inch pastry bag fitted with a number 2 piping tip and filled with green flood consistency icing

Piece of parchment or wax paper

12-inch pastry bag fitted with a number 3 piping tip and filled with slightly thinned, stiff consistency icing

Scribe tool

White nonpareils

COLORS

Blue: Wilton® Delphinium Blue

Green: Wilton® Juniper Green

QUICK TIP

Make the trees ahead of time as royal icing transfers. Follow the instructions on p. 22 and apply the transfers after icing the globe in blue.

TO MAKE THE SNOW GLOBES

1. Cut the snow globes and stands from a chilled sheet of cookie dough using the template and a paring knife. Bake the cookies according to the recipe.

2. Ice the globe portion of the cookie with blue flood consistency icing and a number 3 tip according to the instrutions on p. 17. Immediately add a reflection in the globe by piping a line of white flood consistency icing with a number 3 tip. Start on the top right and bring it down to the bottom right, releasing the pressure toward the end to taper the line.

3. While the blue icing is still wet, place the cookie on the parchment or wax paper and sprinkle the cookie with white nonpareils, concentrating on the bottom of the globe. Let the icing dry about 2 hours.

4. Pipe a tree on the globe with green flood consistency icing and a number 3 tip, and use the scribe tool to help shape the points of the tree. Add a few white nonpareils to the tree.

5. Fill in the base of the cookie with red flood consistency icing and and a number 3 tip. Let the icing dry completely, about 8 hours.

6. Attach the stand to the back of the snow globe with slightly thinned stiff consistency icing and a number 3 tip. Hold the pieces together for about 30 seconds to make sure they stick.

{6}

SPECIAL OCCASIONS

I LOVE MAKING COOKIES AS GIFTS FOR SPECIAL OCCASIONS— birthdays, weddings, showers, and everything in between. Wrap these cookies up in a window box with a pretty bow for a gift that's as beautiful as it is delicious! And who doesn't love an edible party favor? An individually wrapped cookie on each place setting doubles as table decor.

Cookie Cake

This birthday cake looks just like the original, only much smaller! Try mixing and matching colors and flavors to create a birthday treat that's all your own.

YOU'LL NEED

Chocolate cookie dough, p. 120

4-inch round cookie cutter

Paring knife

12-inch pastry bag fitted with a number 2 piping tip and filled with pink flood consistency royal icing

12-inch pastry bags fitted with a number 2 piping tip and filled with blue and green stiff consistency royal icing

12-inch pastry bag fitted with a number18 piping tip and filled with white stiff consistency royal icing

COLORS

Pink: Wilton® Aster Mauve

Blue: Wilton® Delphinium Blue

Green: Wilton® Juniper Green

TO MAKE THE CAKE

1. To make a cake cookie, cut two round cookies from a chilled sheet of dough. Cut each circle into 8 equal pieces with a paring knife before baking. Bake the cookies according to the cookie recipe.

2. Ice 8 of the pieces with pink flood consistency icing and a number 2 tip. Use a zigzag motion on the edges to make the icing look as if it's dripping off the sides of the slices.

3. On the other 8 pieces, pipe a zigzag outline using pink flood consistency icing and a number 2 tip. Place the flooded pieces on top. Let the icing dry about one hour.

4. To make a tiny rose, pipe a small swirl of blue stiff consistency icing with a number 2 tip on top of each "slice" of cake. Pipe two teardrop shaped leaves with green icing stiff consistency icing and a number 2 tip on each side of the rose.

5. Pipe a shell border with white stiff consistency icing according to the instructions on p. 35. Let the icing dry completely.

Bassinet

What better reason to celebrate with cookies than welcoming a new baby? These bassinet cookies have layers of lace and ruffles, giving them a soft, cuddly appearance.

YOU'LL NEED

Un-iced 3-inch round cookies

12-inch pastry bags fitted with number 3 piping tips and filled with pink, blue, green, and white flood consistency royal icing

12-inch pastry bag fitted with a number 1 piping tip and filled with ivory flood consistency royal icing

12-inch pastry bags fitted with number 3 piping tips and filled with white, green, blue, and pink stiff consistency royal icing

Scribe tool

Pastry bag fitted with a number 104 piping tip and filled with white, pink, and blue stiff consistency royal icing

Black edible ink marker

Square tip brush

Small dish of water

Dry paper towel

COLORS

Pink: Wilton® Aster Mauve

Blue: Wilton® Delphinium Blue

Green: Wilton® Juniper Green

Ivory: A touch of AmeriColor® Chocolate Brown + a touch of Wilton® Juniper Green

TO MAKE THE BASSINET

1. Ice the cookies with pink, blue, green or white flood consistency icing and number a 3 tip according to the instructions on p. 17. Let the icing dry about two hours.

2. Pipe a ½-inch semicircle in the center of the cookie with ivory flood consistency icing and a number 1 tip. This is the "face"—move on to the next step to let it dry for several minutes.

3. Using the brush embroidery method on p. 23, make the curtains over the bassinet with white stiff consistency icing and a number 3 tip. Dip the square tip brush into the water and blot it on a dry paper towel before brushing the icing as described on p. 23. Start with the layer closest to the baby's face and work your way out to the edges. Pipe 3 dots of stiff consistency white icing at the top of the cookie where the curtains meet.

4. To make a blanket, pipe a narrow almond shape of flood consistency icing with a number 3 tip in white, blue or pink.

5. Pipe 2 layers of ruffles with white, pink, or blue stiff consistency icing and a number 104 tip as described on p. 35. Start with the layer on the bottom, and then pipe the second layer so that it overlaps the top edge of the first ruffle.

6. Using green or white stiff consistency icing and a number 3 tip, pipe a bead border along the top edge of the ruffle according to the instructions on p. 35.

7. Use a black edible ink marker to draw sleeping eyes on the babies' faces (you can also add a few eyelashes if you like). Let the icing dry completely.

8. Pipe a bow with green, pink, or blue stiff consistency icing and number 3 tip. The bow is made up of two teardrop shapes with the ends facing in, and a dot in the center where the teardrops meet.

Baby Quilts

The puffy look of quilted fabric is easily achievable with a little patience. The addition of tiny icing buttons makes these cute cookies even more adorable!

YOU'LL NEED

Edible ink marker in any color

Un-iced plaque-shape cookies

Un-iced 1-inch round cookies

12-inch pastry bags fitted with number 3 piping tips and filled with pink, blue, green, and white flood consistency icing

Tissue paper

Letters printed on a piece of paper

12-inch pastry bags fitted with number 1 piping tips and filled with pink, blue, green, and white medium consistency icing

Scribe tool

12-inch pastry bags fitted with number 2 piping tips and filled with pink, blue, green, and white flood consistency icing

COLORS

Pink: Wilton® Aster Mauve

Green: Wilton® Juniper Green

Blue: Wilton® Delphinium Blue

QUICK TIP

Save some time by planning ahead. Make the letters using the royal icing transfer method on p. 22 and save them until you're ready to decorate.

TO MAKE THE QUILTS

1. Use the edible ink marker to draw a 2-inch diamond pattern on the plaque-shape cookies. Using the quilting method on p. 20, ice the cookies with pink, green, white or blue flood consistency icing and a number 3 tip. Let the icing dry completely.

2. Using the tissue paper, printed letter, and edible ink marker, draw the letters on the cookies with the Tissue Paper Method shown on p. 21. Pipe over the letters with the white medium consistency icing and a number 1 tip. Use the scribe tool to help shape the icing while it's still wet.

3. To make the tiny buttons on the quilted cookie, pipe a small circle with white medium consistency icing and a number 1 tip. Leave two small holes for the "thread." Let the icing dry about 10 minutes, and then go over the edge of the circle again with the white medium consistency icing to make a rim on the button.

4. For the stitches, pipe ¼-inch lines around the edge of the cookie with medium consistency icing in a contrasting color with a tip 1. Add stitches to the letters, as well. Pipe one stitch in the center of each button.

5. To make the button cookies, ice the 1-inch rounds with flood consistency icing and a number 2 tip, leaving 4 holes in the center. Let the icing to dry about 30 minutes. With the same icing, pipe an outline around the edge of the cookie to create a rim. Use the medium consistency icing and number 1 tip to pipe an "X" stitch in the center.

Bears

The texture and shading here were inspired by the mohair fabric found on vintage teddy bears. These cookies are so cute and fuzzy, you won't know whether to eat them or give them a hug!

YOU'LL NEED

Un-iced teddy-bear-shape cookies

12-inch pastry bag fitted with a number 3 piping tip and filled with light brown flood consistency royal icing

12-inch pastry bag fitted with a number 1 piping tip and filled with ivory flood consistency royal icing

Round brush

Flat angled brush

Dark shade of matte dust, such as Wilton® Brown Color Dust

12-inch pastry bags fitted with number 2 piping tips and filled with pink, blue, and green stiff consistency royal icing

12-inch pastry bag fitted with a number 1 piping tip and filled with black flood consistency royal icing

Scribe tool

COLORS

Light brown: AmeriColor® Chocolate Brown + a touch of Wilton® Juniper Green

Ivory: A touch of Wilton® Buttercup Yellow

Pink: Wilton® Aster Mauve

Blue: Wilton® Delphinium Blue

Green: Wilton® Juniper Green

Black: AmeriColor™ Super Black

TO MAKE THE BEARS

1. Ice the cookie with light brown flood consistency icing and a number 3 tip according to the instrcutions on p. 17. With ivory flood consistency icing and a number 1 tip, immediately pipe small ovals on the bear's paws and ears. Let the icing dry completely, about 8 hours.

2. Using light brown flood consistency icing with a number 3 tip and a round brush, follow the instructions on p. 29 to create a fuzzy texture. Before the icing dries, drag the end of the brush handle through the icing to create "seams" in the bear. Make one seam down the center starting from the neck, one under each ear, and one where each paw meets the bear's body. Let the icing dry about 30 minutes.

3. Using a flat angled brush and a dark shade of matte color dust, add shading all around the bear's edges and seams. (This process is described on p. 30.) Using ivory flood consistency icing and a number 1 tip, pipe the muzzle.

4. Using pink, blue, or green stiff consistency icing and a number 2 tip, add a bow: Pipe a curved line across the bear's neck. Pipe two loops, two ends, and add a dot in the center.

5. Once the muzzle is dry, use black flood consistency icing and a tip 1 to pipe a nose. Using the scribe tool, drag the icing from the nose to create a mouth. Pipe two eyes, starting with a dot of black, then add a dot of ivory, and another dot of black. There should just be a sliver of ivory showing in each eye to give the illusion of a reflection.

Monogram

These blue and white monogram cookies were originally inspired by my Wedgwood® Jasperware collection. The design is one of the very first I made when I started decorating cookies several years ago. Don't worry about piping a monogram freehand—use the Tissue Paper Method on p. 21 to help you along.

YOU'LL NEED

Un-iced 3-inch round cookies

12-inch pastry bag fitted with a number 3 piping tip and filled with dark blue flood consistency royal icing

1½-inch round cookie cutter

Letter printed on a piece of paper

Square of tissue paper large enough to cover the cookie

Edible ink marker in any color

12-inch pastry bag fitted with a number 1 piping tip and filled with white medium consistency royal icing.

Scribe tool

COLOR

Dark blue: Wilton® Delphinium Blue + a touch of AmeriColor® Super Black

TO MAKE THE MONOGRAM

1. Begin by icing a round cookie with blue flood consistency icing and a tip 3 according to the instructions on p. 17. Let the icing dry about 10 minutes and then press the 1½-inch cookie cutter into the icing. When you lift the cutter, it will leave a round outline; if the icing settles and the outline disappears, wait a couple of minutes longer and try again.

2. Once the icing is completely dry, fill in the round outline with the blue icing. Allow the icing to dry completely, about 8 hours.

3. Use the printed letter, square of tissue paper, and edible ink marker to transfer the letter onto the icing. Instructions for this pattern transfer method can be found on p. 21.

4. Pipe over the letter using white medium consistency icing and a number 1 tip. Use the scribe tool to help shape the letter.

5. Add a bead border around the small circle and a double bead border around the edge of the cookie using white medium consistency icing and number 1 tip as described on p. 35.

SAVE TIME BY PLANNING AHEAD

Make the smaller circle with the monogram ahead of time by using the royal icing transfer method shown on p.22. Pipe 1½-inch blue circles on a piece of wax paper, let them dry, and follow the instructions above for making a monogram. When you're ready to decorate, flood the cookie and apply the monogrammed disk.

Hearts with Gold Trim

The beauty of these cookies is in the decoration's simplicity. A little bit of asymmetry in the gold outline gives this design a touch of whimsy.

YOU'LL NEED

Un-iced 3-inch round cookies

Edible ink marker in any color

12-inch pastry bag fitted with a number 3 piping tip and filled with white flood consistency royal icing

12-inch pastry bag fitted with a number 2 piping tip and filled with pink flood consistency royal icing

Scribe tool

12-inch pastry bag fitted with a number 3 piping tip and filled with brown medium consistency royal icing

Gold pearl dust such as Crystal Colors® Antique Gold

Alcohol or flavored extract

Eyedropper

Palette or small dish for mixing pearl dust

Round brush

COLORS

Pink: Wilton® Aster Mauve

Brown: AmeriColor® Chocolate Brown + a touch of Wilton® Juniper Green

TO MAKE THE HEARTS

1. Draw a heart on the cookie using the edible ink marker. The top and the bottom of the heart should end about ¼ inch in from the edge of the cookie.

2. Outline the cookie with white flood consistency icing and a number 3 tip. Immediately fill in the space between the outline and the edge of the heart.

3. While the white icing is still wet, fill in the heart with pink flood consistency icing and number 2 tip. Use the scribe tool to fill in any gaps in the icing, as well as to help shape the heart. Let the icing dry completely, about 8 hours.

4. Using brown medium consistency icing and a number 3 tip, outline the heart, one side at a time, in an asymmetrical fashion. Allow the icing to dry about 30 minutes.

5. Add few drops of alcohol or flavored extract to gold pearl dust with an eyedropper according to the instructions on p. 27. Use a round brush to apply the paint to the outline of the heart.

PRETTY PIPING TIP

When outlining the heart, keep the tip steady for a moment while you squeeze the piping bag to allow the icing to build up at the top and bottom of the design. This will give you varying thickness in the lines, much like the filigree design shown on p. 48.

Eyelet Lace

The delicate patterns of eyelet lace fabric were just waiting to be turned into a beautiful cookie! You can make each cookie look the same, or as I like to do, decorate each one with a different pattern. If you're feeling apprehensive about drawing patterns freehand on the cookies, try sketching them on paper first.

YOU'LL NEED

Un-iced 4-inch scallop-edge cookies, cut in half before baking

Yellow edible ink marker

Scribe tool

Pastry bag fitted with a number 2 piping tip and filled with white flood consistency royal icing

Pastry bag fitted with a number 1 piping tip and filled with white medium consistency royal icing

DRESS IT UP!

Add a brush embroidered border around the edges of the cookie with stiff consistency royal icing and a number 1 piping tip. You can find instructions for the brush embroidery technique on p. 23.

TO MAKE THE EYELET LACE

1. Draw a pattern of circles and teardrops on a scallop-edge cookie with a yelllow edible ink marker.

2. Fill in the space around the pattern with white flood consistency icing and number 2 tip. Let the icing dry about 4 hours.

3. Outline all of the open spaces with white medium consistency icing and number 1 tip. This will help to make the lace look more realistic.

4. Pipe an array of decorations on the cookies, such as swags, beads, fleur-de-lis, and dots using white medium consistency icing and number 1 tip. You can make these as simple or as elaborate as you please.

Fondant Cameos
& Brush Embroidery

This cookie set combines two of my favorite designs: fondant cameos and brush embroidered flowers. A dusting of bronze pearl dust around the cameo cookies adds to the vintage look of these beauties.

YOU'LL NEED

Un-iced 4-inch fancy plaque cookies

Un-iced 3x3-inch square cookies

12-inch pastry bag fitted with a number 3 piping tip and filled with blue flood consistency royal icing

FOR THE BRUSH EMBROIDERED COOKIE

Scribe tool

Flower template, p. 134

12-inch pastry bag fitted with a number 2 tip and filled with ivory stiff consistency royal icing

12-inch pastry bag fitted with a number 3 tip and filled with white stiff consistency royal icing

White pearl dust

Alcohol or flavored extract

Eyedropper

Palette for mixing pearl dust

Round brush

Square tip brush

Small dish of water

Dry paper towel

FOR THE CAMEO COOKIE

Fondant cameo mold (I made mine with a cameo and food-safe mold-making material)

½-inch ball of white fondant

1. Ice both the fancy plaque and square cookies with blue flood consistency icing and number 3 tip according to the instructions on p. 17. Let the icing dry completely, about 8 hours.

TO MAKE THE BRUSH EMBROIDERED FLOWERS
2. Use the scribe tool to trace the flower template onto the square cookie. Follow the instructions on p. 23 to create brush embroidered flowers using ivory stiff consistency icing with a number 2 tip and a square tip brush. Dip the brush into the dish of water and blot it on the dry paper towel before brushing the icing as described on p. 23. Using white stiff consistency icing and number 3 tip, pipe dots and a bead border according to the instructions on p.35.

TO MAKE THE CAMEO
3. Press a small amount of fondant into the bottom of the mold dusted with cornstarch so that only the cameo bust is filled in (don't fill the mold all the way to the top). Use the scribe tool to push the fondant into any tiny crevices around the edge of the cameo, such as the nose. Immediately remove the cameo from the mold as shown on p. 25 and apply it to the plaque cookie using a dab of brown medium consistency icing.

4. Pipe a bead border around the cameo using brown medium consistency icing and number 1 tip. Then, make a double bead border according to the instructions on p. 35, leaving about 1 inch open at the top. Pipe 3 tear drop shapes in each corner on the cookie for a little added elegance. Pipe a bead border around the edge of the cookie with white stiff consistency icing and number 3 tip. Let the icing dry about 30 minutes.

5. Lightly brush the cameo and the space inside the small bead

Cornstarch

Scribe tool

12-inch pastry bag fitted with a number 1 piping tip and filled with brown medium consistency royal icing

12-inch pastry bag fitted with a number 3 piping tip and filled with white stiff consistency royal icing

Bronze pearl dust

Flat angled brush

Gold pearl dust such as Crystal Colors™ Antique Gold

White pearl dust

Alcohol or flavored extract

Eyedropper

Palette for mixing pearl dust

Soft round brush

COLORS

Blue: Wilton® Delphinium Blue

Ivory: A touch of AmeriColor® Chocolate Brown + a touch of Wilton® Juniper Green

border with bronze pearl dust using a flat angled brush. Dust the edges of the cookie, as well. This will give the cookie an antique look.

6. Add a few drops of alcohol or flavored extract to gold pearl dust according to the instructions on p. 27. Paint the brown borders gold using a round brush. Repeat this process on the white borders and dots on both cookies using white pearl dust.

QUICK TIP

Use round cookie cutters as guides to pipe the borders around the cameo. Place the cookie cutter on top of the icing after it's completely dry and trace it with the scribe tool.

Hand-Painted Tea Set with Brush Embroidered Border

These Delftware-inspired treats make me want to have a tea party! Don't be intimidated by the tiny tea cups and tea pots in this set of cookies. The template on p. 137 makes it easy to pipe a perfect tea set.

YOU'LL NEED

Tea set template, p. 137

12-inch pastry bag fitted with a number 1 piping tip and filled with white medium consistency icing

Wax paper wrapped around a cake board or sheet tray for piping royal icing transfers

Blue gel paste food coloring

Alcohol or flavored extract

Eyedropper

Fine tip brush

Palette (or small dish) for mixing gel paste paint

Un-iced 2½-inch round cookies

12-inch pastry bag fitted with a number 3 piping tip and filled with blue flood consistency royal icing

2-inch round cookie cutter to use as a guide

Scribe tool

Pastry bag fitted with a number 2 piping tip and filled with white stiff consistency royal icing

Square tip brush

Small dish of water

Dry paper towel

COLOR

Blue: Wilton® Delphinium Blue

TO MAKE THE TEA POTS AND CUPS

1. Follow the instructions on p. 22 to make royal icing transfers on a board wrapped with wax paper using the tea set template and white medium consistency icing with a number 1 tip. Let the transfers dry completely, about 8 hours.

2. Add a few drops of alcohol or flavored extract to blue gel paste food coloring in the palette or small dish to form an edible paint. Use a fine tip brush to paint flowers and dots on the royal icing transfers as described on p. 27. The color should be dry within a few minutes. Gently remove the transfers from the wax paper according to the instructions on p. 22.

3. Ice a round cookie with blue flood consistency icing and a number 3 tip according to the instructions on p. 17. Place a teapot or teacup icing transfer in the center of the cookie. Let the icing dry completely, about 8 hours.

4. Place the 2-inch round cookie cutter in the center of the cookie and trace it with the scribe tool to make a guide for the brush embroidered border.

5. To make the border, pipe a ruffled line with white stiff consistency icing and number 2 tip on the edge of the blue icing. Dip the square tip brush into the dish of water and blot it on a dry paper towel and brush the icing inward as shown on p. 23. Work in small sections so that the icing doesn't dry before you have a chance to brush it.

6. Pipe a bead border along the inside edge of the brush embroidery with white stiff consistency icing and number 3 tip according to the instructions on p. 35.

7. Apply the tea set transfers to the cookies using a dab of white medium consistency icing used to make the transfers.

Cracked Glaze Tea Set

The Cracked Glaze Technique, p. 28, gives royal icing a realistic looking porcelain effect. Combined with wet-on-wet roses and a little gold trim, these charming treats are almost too pretty to eat!

YOU'LL NEED

Un-iced teacup- and teapot-shape cookies or un-iced 3-inch round cookies

12-inch pastry bags fitted with number 3 tips and filled with white flood consistency royal icing

12-inch pastry bag fitted with a number 2 piping tip and filled with light pink flood consistency royal icing

12-inch pastry bag fitted with a number 1 piping tip and filled with dark pink flood consistency royal icing

12-inch pastry bag fitted with a number 1 piping tip and filled with light green flood consistency royal icing

12-inch pastry bag fitted with a number 1 piping tip and filled with dark green flood consistency royal icing

Scribe tool

Dark shade of matte dust, such as Wilton® Brown Color Dust

Round brush

12-inch pastry bag fitted with a number 1 tip and filled with brown medium consistency icing

Gold pearl dust, such as Crystal Colors™ Antique Gold

Alcohol or flavored extract

Eyedropper

Palette or small dish for mixing pearl dust

COLORS

Pink: Wilton® Aster Mauve

Green: Wilton® Juniper Green

Brown: AmeriColor® Chocolate Brown + a touch of Wilton Juniper Green

TO MAKE THE TEA SET

1. Ice a teacup-, teapot-shape or round cookie with white flood consistency icing and a number 3 tip according to the instructions on p. 17. Using the Wet-On-Wet Rose Technique on p. 18, immediately pipe a rose in the center of the cookie with light pink, dark pink, light green, and dark green icing flood consistency icings. Let the icing dry about 20 minutes, and then add a handle with the white icing. Allow the icing to dry completely, about 8 hours.

2. Use the scribe tool to scratch the surface of the icing, leaving a narrow almond shape at the top of the teacup cookie without scratches. Using a dark shade of matte dust and a round brush, follow the instructions for the Cracked Glaze Technique on p. 28 to complete the antiquing process.

3. Dust the top portion of the teacup that was left blank earlier with the matte dust and a round brush. Concentrate the dust on one side to give the illusion of depth.

4. With brown icing medium consistency icing and a number 1 tip, pipe an outline around the top edge and just above the bottom rim of the teacup, as well as on the spout and bottom of the teapot's lid, and all the way around the edge of the round cookie.

5. Add a few drops of alcohol or flavored extract to gold pearl dust with an eyedropper according to the instructions on p. 27. Use the round brush to apply the gold paint to the brown icing.

QUICK TIP

Make sure to ice only one cookie at a time when working with the wet-on-wet technique. If you try to ice all of the cookies in white at once and then go back and add the roses, the white icing will be too dry to work with.

{7}

PRETTY PASTRIES

ONE OF THE GREATEST THINGS ABOUT ROYAL ICING AND fondant decorations is that they can be made ahead of time, so they're available whenever you need a pretty dessert in a pinch. You don't need to reserve these beauties just for cookies–they're equally stunning on cupcakes, cakes, and brownies.

Cupcakes

Whip up a batch of your favorite chocolate cupcakes and top them with a sweet and smooth cream cheese frosting. No time to bake from scratch? A boxed mix will do! Top these party favorites with a make-ahead royal icing rose transfer, which will dress up a plain cupcake in no time.

YOU'LL NEED

Your favorite cupcake recipe or boxed cake mix

Cream cheese frosting, p. 127

12-inch pastry bag fitted with a large round decorating tip (or cut a 1/2-inch hole in the tip of the bag) and filled with dark pink cream cheese frosting

1-inch pre-made royal icing rose transfers (see p. 22 and p. 18)

9" metal spatula

COLORS

Blue: Wilton® Delphinium Blue

Dark and Light Pink: Wilton® Aster Mauve

Green: Wilton® Juniper Green

TO MAKE THE CUPCAKES

1. To make a royal icing rose transfer, use the royal icing transfer method on p. 22 and the wet-on-wet rose technique on p. 18. Let the icing dry completely before applying the transfers to the cupcakes, about 8 hours.

2. Bake and cool your favorite cupcake recipe. Ice the cupcakes using a spiral motion, starting from the outside and working your way toward the center. Use the 9-inch metal spatula to smooth the icing.

4. Place the royal icing rose transfer on top of the iced cupcake before serving.

QUICK TIP

Royal icing transfers can be made several weeks ahead and stored in an airtight container until you're ready to use them. Any time you have some extra royal icing after decorating cookies, you can make some of these to have on hand for later.

Cake

This cake is modeled after one that I made for my cousin on her thirtieth birthday. Adorning a spatula-iced cake with pre-made royal icing roses is a quick way to add a little more charm to a beautiful rustic dessert.

YOU'LL NEED

Pre-made royal icing roses and leaves, p. 24

Your favorite cake recipe or boxed cake mix

Buttercream frosting, p. 125

9-inch metal spatula

COLORS

Pink: Wilton® Aster Mauve

Green: Wilton® Juniper Green

TO MAKE THE POLKA DOTS

1. Follow the instructions on p. 24 to make piped roses and leaves and let the icing dry completely. The leaves can be piped separately onto a sheet of waxed paper to dry before arranging them on the cake.

2. Bake and cool your favorite cake recipe or boxed cake mix according to the instructions.

Apply the buttercream frosting to the cake with the 9-inch metal spatula. Once the cake is completely covered, mark the cake with the spatula for a rustic look.

3. Attach the roses on the sides and top of the cake with a dab of buttercream before serving. Place two leaves on either side of the roses.

BUTTERCREAM ROSES

Royal icing roses are crunchy, so if you prefer to have a soft decoration, you can make these piped roses using buttercream instead. You won't be able to store them and use them later as you would with the royal icing rose, of course, but they're just as pretty.

Brownies

We all know that brownies are delicious, but they can be pretty, too! Scatter some of these pale pink rose petals on them for an extra special treat.

YOU'LL NEED

Your favorite brownie recipe or boxed brownie mix

Pre-made fondant rose petals, p. 26

12-inch pastry bag fitted with a number 18 star piping tip and filled with cream cheese frosting, p. 127

QUICK TIP

Your rose petals will have a more natural look if they're slightly curled. See p. 26 for a tip on how to do it.

TO MAKE THE BROWNIES

1. Follow the instructions on p. 26 to make fondant rose petals. You can use them right away or let them dry them overnight to save for another time.

2. Bake and cool the brownies. Cut them into the desired serving size and place the fondant rose petals on top of and around each one. Pipe a dollop of cream cheese frosting on top of the each brownie with a star tip number 18 to prop up a single rose petal.

{ PART THREE }

THE
RECIPES

{8}

RECIPES

TO MAKE A GREAT DECORATED COOKIE, YOU NEED TO START WITH

the right recipes! The cookie recipes in this chapter are the three that

I use most often for making decorated cookies. I've also provided my

royal icing recipe, plus recipes for simple buttercream and a delicious

cream cheese frosting, both of which can be used on your favorite cakes,

cupcakes, or brownies.

Orange Vanilla Spice Cookies

This is my original cookie recipe, and my all-time favorite—the cookies aren't too sweet, hold their shape while baking, and taste incredible. Soft on the inside and crunchy around the edges, they're perfectly balanced by the crisp texture of the royal icing. This recipe uses agave syrup, a lightly flavored liquid sweetener, which helps to retain the moisture. If you can't find it, you can use honey instead; the flavor will be slightly different, but the texture of the cookie will remain the same. If you live in a humid climate, the agave syrup or honey could make your cookies too soft, so try replacing it with the same amount of granulated sugar.

YIELDS ABOUT 3 DOZEN 3-INCH COOKIES.

4 cups (575 grams) all-purpose flour; plus more for dusting

1 tsp. (4 grams) baking powder

1 tsp. (2 grams) ground cardamom

1 tsp. (4 grams) salt

1 cup (226 grams) unsalted butter, softened

1-¾ cup (350 grams) granulated sugar

¼ cup (70 grams) agave syrup

Zest of 1 medium orange (about 2 Tbs.)

2 tsp. (10 mL) pure vanilla extract

2 large eggs, room temperature

2-3 Tbs. (29.5-44.25 mL) milk, as needed

1. Sift the flour, baking powder, cardamom, and salt into a medium bowl. Whisk to combine.

2. In large bowl, beat the butter and sugar with an electric mixer (handheld, or a stand mixer fitted with the paddle attachment) on medium speed until the mixture is light and fluffy, about 5 minutes. Scrape down the bowl and beater with a rubber spatula as needed. Add the agave syrup and beat on low speed until well blended, about 1 minute more.

3. Add the orange zest and vanilla and continue to beat on low speed until well blended.

4. Add one of the eggs and beat on low speed until well blended. Stop the mixer, scrape the bowl, add the second egg, and beat until well blended.

5. Add the dry ingredients and beat on low speed, stopping once to scrape the bowl, until they're incorporated and the dough pulls away from the sides of the bowl, about 15 seconds. Do not overmix. The dough should be soft and somewhat sticky, but not so sticky that it's difficult to handle. If the dough feels too soft, add flour until it stiffens up (2 Tbs. at a time) If the dough is very dry and crumbly, add 2 to 3 Tbs. milk to soften it.

6. Divide the dough in half and roll each half into a 1-inch-thick rectangle. Wrap each half tightly in plastic and chill the dough for at least 1 hour in the refrigerator. You can also freeze the dough for later use; the dough will stay in the freezer for up to 3 months.

7. Remove the dough from the refrigerator and let soften slightly for 15 to 20 minutes. Roll the dough on a floured sheet of parchment or wax paper to ³⁄₁₆ inch thick. Layer the dough on a baking sheet and chill for another 30 minutes.

8. Position racks in the upper and lower third of the oven and heat the oven to 350°F. Line two or more rimmed baking sheets with parchment or nonstick baking liners.

9. Cut the cookies into the desired shapes while the dough is cold and arrange the cutouts on the prepared pans. Freeze until firm, another 15 minutes.

10. Bake two pans at a time, rotating and switching their positions halfway through, until the cookies' edges are a light golden brown, 10 to 12 minutes. Keep in mind that the cookies will spread slightly, but not so much that they lose their shape. Meanwhile, press the dough scraps together, re-roll, chill, and cut more shapes; freeze. Repeat until all of the dough is used. Cool the cookies completely on a rack before decorating.

FLAVOR VARIATIONS

If orange vanilla spice isn't your style, you can experiment with your own flavor combinations. Try taking out the cardamom and adding some lemon zest in place of the orange. You could also skip the citrus altogether and add ½ tsp. almond extract. Yum!

Chocolate Cookies

If chocolate is more to your liking, this delicious cookie is sure to satisfy. It's one of my favorites!

4 cups. (575 grams) all-purpose flour; plus more for dusting

1 cup (85 grams) cocoa powder

1 tsp. (4grams) salt

1 cup (226 grams) unsalted butter, softened

2 cups (450 grams) granulated sugar

2 large eggs, at room temperature

1 tsp. (5mL) pure vanilla extract

½ cup (122 grams) whole milk, plus more as needed

1. Sift the flour, cocoa powder and salt into a medium bowl. Whisk to combine.

2. In large bowl, beat the butter and sugar with an electric mixer (handheld, or a stand mixer fitted with the paddle attachment) on medium speed until the mixture is light and fluffy, about 5 minutes. Scrape down the bowl and beater with a rubber spatula as needed.

4. Add one egg and mix on low speed until it's well blended. Stop the mixer, scrape the bowl, add the second egg, and beat until well blended. Add the vanilla and milk and beat until well blended.

5. Add the dry ingredients and beat on low speed, stopping once to scrape the bowl, until they're incorporated and the dough pulls away from the sides of the bowl, about 15 seconds. Do not overmix. The dough should be soft and somewhat sticky, but not so sticky that it's difficult to handle. If the dough feels too soft, add flour until it stiffens up (2 Tbs. at a time). If the dough is very dry and crumbly, add another 2 to 3 Tbs. milk to soften it.

6. Divide the dough in half and roll each half into a 1-inch-thick rectangle. Wrap each half tightly in plastic and chill the dough for at least 1 hour in refrigerator. You can also freeze the dough for later use; the dough can last in the freezer for up to 3 months.

7. Remove the dough from the refrigerator and let it soften slightly for 15 to 20 minutes. Roll the dough on a floured sheet of parchment or wax paper to ³⁄₁₆ inch thick. Layer the dough on a baking sheet and chill for another 30 minutes.

8. Position racks in the upper and lower third of the oven and heat the oven to 350°F. Line two or more rimmed baking sheets with parchment or nonstick baking liners.

9. Cut the cookies into the desired shapes while the dough is cold and arrange the cutouts on the prepared pans. Freeze until firm, another 15 minutes.

10. Bake two pans at a time, rotating and switching their positions halfway through, for 10 to 12 minutes. Meanwhile, press the dough scraps together, re-roll, chill, and cut more shapes; freeze. Repeat until all of the dough is used. Cool the cookies completely on a rack before decorating.

TIPS ON MAKING COOKIE DOUGH

When decorating cookies with royal icing, it's important that you start with cookies that have a nice flat, smooth surface. To ensure that your cookies come out this way, here are a few tips.

1. Keep the mixing to a minimum. Dough that's overmixed can lead to a tough texture and can cause cookies to shrink and become misshapen in the oven. Overhandling the dough can lead to the same problem, so it's also a good idea to only re-roll scraps twice. On the last roll, cut your cookies into squares to reduce waste. If you don't need square cookies for whatever you're working on, freeze and use them another time, or cut them up, pop them into the oven, and pass them out as tasting samples.

2. Work with the dough while it's cold. Warm, soft dough becomes sticky and hard to handle, which is not only frustrating, but your cookies will be less likely to hold their shape. Make sure to cut cookies only out of chilled sheets of dough, even if this means working with one sheet of dough at a time while the others wait in the refrigerator.

3. If you're using a recipe that's not in this book and your cookies are spreading while baking, try reducing the amount of baking powder. A little bit of baking powder in a cookie is necessary for a pleasant texture, but too much can cause the cookies to become rounded on top and around the edges.

Gingerbread Cookies

There's nothing like baking gingerbread cookies for the holidays! This cookie recipe, like the others in this book, is perfect for decorating. It holds its shape, isn't overly sweet, and the scent of these baking in the oven is sure to get you in the holiday spirit.

5 cups (718 grams) all-purpose flour; plus more for dusting

½ tsp. (2 grams) baking powder

2 tsp. (8 grams) ground ginger

1 tsp. (4 grams) ground cinnamon

1 tsp. (4 grams) salt

½ tsp. (2 grams) ground allspice

½ tsp. (2 grams) ground cloves

½ tsp. (2 grams) ground nutmeg

1 cup (226 grams) unsalted butter, softened

1 cup (225 grams) granulated sugar

1 cup (340 grams) molasses

2 large eggs, at room temperature

1. Sift the flour, baking powder, ginger, cinnamon, salt, allspice, cloves, and nutmeg into a medium bowl. Whisk to combine.

2. In a large bowl, beat the sugar and butter with an electric mixer (handheld, or a stand mixer fitted with the paddle attachment) on medium speed until the mixture is light and fluffy, about 5 minutes. Scrape down the bowl and beater with a rubber spatula as needed. Add the molasses and beat on low speed until well blended, about 1 minute more.

4. Add one egg and mix on low speed until it's well blended. Stop the mixer, scrape the bowl, add the second egg, and beat until well blended.

5. Add the dry ingredients beat on low speed, stopping once to scrape the bowl, until they're incorporated and the dough pulls away from the sides of the bowl, about 15 seconds. Do not overmix. This dough will be softer than the dough in the other two cookie recipes in this book. If the dough is very sticky and difficult to handle, add flour until it stiffens up (2 Tbs. at a time).

6. Divide the dough in half and roll each half into a 1-inch-thick thick rectangle. Wrap each half tightly in plastic and chill the dough for at least 1 hour in refrigerator. You can also freeze the dough for later use; the dough will stay in the freezer about 3 months.

7. Remove the dough from the refrigerator and let it soften slightly for 15 to 20 minutes. Roll the dough on a floured sheet of parchment or wax paper to ³⁄₁₆ inch thick. Layer the dough on baking sheet and chill for another 30 minutes.

8. Position racks in the upper and lower third of the oven and heat the oven to 350ºF. Line two or more rimmed baking sheet with parchment or nonstick baking liners.

9. With a floured cookie cutter, cut the cookies while the dough is cold and arrange the cutouts on the prepared pans. Freeze until firm, another 15 minutes.

10. Bake two pans at a time, rotating and switching their positions halfway through, for 10 to 12 minutes. Keep in mind that the cookies will spread slightly, but not so much that they lose their shape. Meanwhile, press the dough scraps together, re-roll, chill, and cut more shapes; freeze. Repeat until all of the dough is used. Cool the cookies completely on a rack before decorating.

HOW TO HANDLE LARGE QUANTITIES OF COOKIES

Decorated cookies make fantastic personalized favors for weddings and special events. It can seem overwhelming to handle a large order of cookies, but if you break it down into steps, it's much more manageable.

Save time later by cutting the cookies and freezing them raw up to three months in advance. As you cut out the cookies, stack them with parchment paper in between each layer. Place the sheets in the freezer to chill until the raw cookies are hard, 15 to 30 minutes. Remove them from the freezer, stack them in sets of 8 (no need for parchment in between once they're frozen solid), and wrap each stack tightly in plastic wrap. Then, when it's time to bake, just remove them from the freezer, unwrap them, transfer them to a room temperature baking sheet, and put them in the oven. No need to thaw!

I wrap my cookies in sets of 8 because that's how many I can fit on a baking sheet in the oven (two rows of 3 and one row of 2 in the middle), but you can stack them however you'd like. You can also just leave them on baking sheets and wrap the whole thing in plastic, but it saves more room in the freezer to consolidate the raw cookies.

Start decorating a week or two ahead of the event, depending on whether you're shipping the cookies. If you're shipping them, I'd recommend starting two weeks ahead to give yourself an extra week of time in transit. To keep things organized, I like to bake and decorate up to 4 dozen cookies at a time. Once those 4 dozen cookies are finished, I wrap them up in cellophane bags, seal them with a heat sealer to keep them fresh and put them aside to make room for the next 4 dozen. Once the cookies are wrapped and sealed, they'll stay fresh for 3 to 4 weeks, giving you plenty of time to finish the entire order. Decorating in small batches keeps things running smoothly and saves a lot of room, since all 100-plus cookies aren't laying out on baking sheets at one time.

Royal Icing

The royal icing that is used to decorate the cookies throughout this book dries with a smooth finish, has a crispy texture, and the best part is that it's incredibly versatile. This recipe makes stiff consistency icing. See p. 13 for information on thinning the icing down to make medium and flood consistency.

This recipe makes enough royal icing to decorate about 3-½ dozen 3-inch cookies.

YIELDS ABOUT 4½ CUPS

7 ½ cups (910 grams) confectioners sugar

½ cup plus 2 tablespoons (104 grams) meringue powder

Pinch salt

¾ cups (177 mL) water, room temperature, plus more for thinning

2 tsp. (10 mL) pure vanilla extract

1. In stand mixer fitted with the paddle attachment, beat the confectioners' sugar, meringue powder, and salt on low speed until combined.

2. Still on low speed, add the water to the dry ingredients, but don't add it all at once. Depending on the humidity, you might not need the full ¾ cup. Hold back about ¼ cup at first, then add more water if the mixture is dry and crumbly. Add the vanilla extract and mix on low speed until combined. Once all of the dry ingredients are moistened, turn the mixer off and scrape the bowl.

3. Continue to mix the icing on low speed until the icing is light in color and holds a stiff peak, 3 to 5 minutes. It's very important that you don't overmix the icing (see p. 129 for more information on that).

4. Use this stiff consistency icing as-is, or add more water to create flood or medium consistency icing (see p. 13 for more information on icing consistency). To save the icing for later, transfer it to a container, cover with a layer of plastic film touching the surface, and cover securely with a lid. Refrigerate for up to 10 days. Mix the icing well by hand when you're ready to use it.

QUICK TIP

You can experiment with flavors by adding extracts to your royal icing. Stay away from citrus flavors though, as royal icng is already tart on its own.

Buttercream Frosting

This super simple buttercream recipe is a yummy topping for your favorite cakes and cupcakes. You can experiment with flavors by swapping in other extracts, such as almond, peppermint, or orange. This recipe decorates about 18 to 24 cupcakes or one 8-inch cake.

YIELDS ABOUT 3 CUPS

1 cup (226 grams) unsalted butter, softened

4 cups (500 grams) confectioners' sugar

1 Tbs. (15 mL) pure vanilla extract

¼ tsp. (1 gram) salt

2 Tbs. (29.5 mL) whole milk

1. In a large bowl, beat the butter with an electric mixer (either handheld, or a stand mixer fitted with the paddle attachment) on medium speed until smooth, about 5 minutes.

2. Still on low speed low speed, add the confectioners' sugar 1 cup at a time, mixing thoroughly and stopping to scrape the bowl between additions.

3. Add the vanilla, milk and salt and continue to beat on medium speed until the frosting is light and fluffy, about 2 minutes.

Cream Cheese Frosting

Cream cheese frosting tastes great on just about anything. I love it on chocolate cupcakes and brownies, but it's also amazing sandwiched between two chocolate cookies. For this recipe, make sure the butter is softened; if it's the least bit cold, the frosting will be lumpy. This recipe decorates about 18 to 24 cupcakes or one 8-inch cake.

YIELDS ABOUT 3 CUPS

1 cup (226 grams) cream cheese, softened

½ cup (113 grams) unsalted butter, softened

4 cups (500 grams) confectioners' sugar

1 tsp. (5 mL) pure vanilla extract

¼ tsp. (1 gram) salt

1. In a large bowl, beat the cream cheese with an electric mixer (handheld, or a stand mixer fitted with the paddle attachment) on medium speed until smooth, about 5 minutes.

2. Still on medium speed, add the butter about 2 Tbs. at a time, and continue to beat until smooth, about 2 more minutes.

3. With the mixer on low speed, add the confectioners' sugar (1 cup at a time), vanilla, and salt and beat on high until the frosting is fluffy, 2 to 3 minutes more.

MEASURING

When measuring the flour and sugar, I use a metal or plastic measuring cup to scoop the flour out of the container and then level it off with a spatula, rather than scooping the flour into the measuring cup with a spoon.

APPENDIX

Royal Icing Troubleshooting Tips

While royal icing can be a lot of fun to work with, it can also be frustrating. If you run into trouble while decorating with it, here are some tips to help you out.

Mixing

This first step when making royal icing is the most important. To prevent the mixer from incorporating too much air into the icing, make sure to mix it no longer than 5 minutes on a low speed, such as 1 or 2. If you have a stand mixer, use the paddle attachment rather than the whisk. Check the icing after 3 minutes of mixing—if it's light in color, thick like cream cheese, and holds a peak, it's ready. Overmixed icing can lead to a slew of problems, such as air bubbles, color bleed, inability to hold its shape (this is especially frustrating when trying to make a 3 dimensional decoration, such as a piped rose), dull finish, fragility, and general unhappiness. If you notice that your icing seems "foamy" as you're using it, it has probably been overmixed.

Drying

Drying the icing as quickly as possible will ensure a smooth, shiny finish on your cookies. Icing that dries very slowly can become porous, which can cause of a number of problems, including a dull finish. In humid climates, it's best to work in an air-conditioned room. If this isn't possible, putting the cookies directly in front of a fan while they dry will help immensely. Even when the weather is cool and dry, I always put my cookies in front of a fan for at least one hour just to be on

the safe side.

Drying times

Drying times for icing can vary depending on the weather as well as the amount of icing that needs to dry. I normally allow my flooded cookies to dry, spread out on baking sheets, for 8 hours before adding any more decoration. The same goes for royal icing transfers, which need to be completely dry before being removed from the waxed paper. However, a drying time of 2 hours for flood-iced cookies in front of a fan can be sufficient depending on what will be happening to the cookies next. If the next step in the process requires you to put pressure on the surface of the cookie (the Cracked Glaze Technique on p. 28, for example), it's best to wait the full 8 hours for the flood icing to dry. If the next step in the process doesn't require you to put pressure on the surface (applying roses or piping filigree, for example), then it's okay to decorate the cookie after just a couple of hours, but make sure to let the icing dry the full 8 hours before packaging the cookies.

Detailed decorations made with medium consistency or stiff consistency icing, such as filigree, brush embroidery, and bead borders, will need less time to dry, since the water content is much lower. Allow 30 minutes to 1 hour for these types of decorations to dry before painting or packaging the cookies.

Once the cookies are completely decorated and ready for packaging, wait the full 8 hours from flood to finish before wrapping them up.

Testing if the icing is dry

If you're new to working with royal icing and not sure how to tell if the icing is dry, make a test cookie with every batch. Ice the test cookie the same way you ice the others. When you're ready to check if the icing is dry, look to see if the icing has lost its gloss. The surface should be somewhat dull, with a bit of a shine around the edges. If the icing looks dry, gently run your finger along the edge of the test cookie. If it feels dry, give the center of the cookie a light tap. If it sounds hollow and the surface doesn't crack, it's most likely dry enough to move on to the next step in the decorating process. After a while, as you become more comfortable working with royal icing, you'll be able to skip the test cookie.

Icing that's too thin

When thinning down your icing to make medium or flood consistency, it's easy to accidentally add too much water. Thin icing can lead to slow drying, which leads to porous icing, which can lead to color bleed as well as butter bleed (read on for more about those cookie conundrums). If your icing is too thin, take a scoop of stiff icing and mix it into the thin icing to thicken it up. I don't recommend adding plain confectioners' sugar to the icing, since that will offset the sugar-to-meringue-powder ratio.

If you accidentally add too much water in the beginning and the stiff consistency icing is not holding a peak, measure 1 lb. confectioners' sugar, add 5 Tbs. meringue powder, and mix well. Add this mixture a spoonful at a time to the icing and mix by hand (or use a mixer on the lowest speed)

until it reaches the correct consistency. Keep some of this dry mixture on hand in the pantry in case you need it for another time. See p. 13 for information on royal icing consistencies.

Icing that won't dry

If you've left your freshly iced cookies out overnight, and in the morning the icing is still not dry (or looks dry at first glance but seems to have a "sandy" texture), there's a problem. There are a few things that might cause this to happen.

The first is overmixing. Those tiny air bubbles in the icing can cause it to become extremely porous, giving the icing a sandy texture. The cookies are still edible of course, but I wouldn't recommend trying to put any more decoration on them or package them because the icing will be very fragile and it will crumble easily.

Another factor that can contribute to icing not drying properly is adding too much color. When you're making a dark shade, such as black, brown, or red, follow the instructions on p. 14 to ensure that your icing has just the right amount of gel paste food coloring. Icing with too much coloring

---

PATIENCE IS KEY

Eight hours might seem like a lot of time to wait for icing to dry, but if you have several cookies to decorate, it's best to spread the project out into smaller steps. I prefer to ice all of my cookies with a layer of flood icing in one day and get to work on the details the following day once the flood icing is dry. If you're in a big hurry, placing the cookies into a dehydrator for 30 minutes can help the process along. However, because of the dehydrator's heat, this isn't my first choice for drying icing. See the section on butter bleed for more information on how heat affects decorated cookies.

can take up to two days to dry, and once it does dry, the surface will be blotchy and pitted. If you think you've added too much color before you ice your cookies, you can remedy the problem by adding more plain white icing.

Decorating cookies in a humid environment can be somewhat of a nightmare. Humidity not only affects the icing, but it can also cause your cookies to become too soft to handle. If you live in a humid climate and your icing isn't drying, keep a fan on them for several hours rather than the 1 or 2 hours I normally recommend. You can also pop the iced cookies into a low oven for a few minutes to help dry them out, but be careful of butter bleed (read on for more on butter bleed).

Color bleed

When you're decorating with two or more colors at one time, there's always the risk that the colors will bleed into each other as the icing dries. To prevent this, use as little color as possible when tinting the icing. See p. 14 for my recommendations on making dark colors. Working with icing that's too thin can also cause color bleed. Thin icing has a tendency to run, and it brings the colors along with it. Make sure that the icing is the correct consistency before you start decorating your cookies.

Butter bleed

Butter bleed is the name for those greasy looking stains that happen in warm weather (or under a heat vent in the winter, which has happened to me!). This occurs when the butter from the cookie melts and seeps into the royal icing. There's no remedy for this, only cover-ups. You can prevent butter bleed by keeping the cookies cool and dry, and making sure that the icing isn't too thin before you begin decorating. Thin icing can contribute to butter bleed, since the more slowly the icing dries, the more porous it becomes,

and the better chance the butter has of seeping through.

If you're experiencing butter bleed, you can cover the stains with icing decorations, or leave the cookie alone and hope that the butter bleed continues to cover the entire surface of the cookie for a more even appearance.

Air bubbles

Air bubbles might not be noticeable at first, but after you've iced a dozen cookies and walked away to check your email, you might come back to see the surface of your cookies covered in tiny dark spots. To prevent air bubbles, make sure that when you're making the icing you don't overmix it. Also, keep the flood consistency icing on the thick side, since thin icing has a tendency to leak air bubbles. If you haven't overmixed the icing and it's the correct consistency, you can still err on the side of caution by allowing the flood consistency icing to sit, covered in a container for an hour or so, to let the air bubbles come to the top. Then, when you're ready to fill the pastry bag, gently paddle the bubbles out with a spatula. While you're icing the cookies, keep a close eye out for air bubbles and use the scribe tool or a toothpick to pop them as they rise to the surface.

My Favorite Suppliers & Brands

Decorating Supplies

Cookie cutters
Ann Clark Cookie Cutters (www.annclarkcookiecutters.com)
Copper Gifts (www.coppergifts.com)

Baking and decorating tools, including food coloring, brushes, pearl dusts, matte dusts, sprinkles, pastry bags, decorating tips, bag ties, baking sheets and parchment paper
Michaels® (www.michaels.com)
Wilton® (www.wilton.com)

Pre-made fondant molds
Etsy® (www.etsy.com)

Specialty decorating products, including pearl dusts, scribe tools, brushes, food coloring and edible ink markers
Global Sugar Art (www.globalsugarart.com)
N.Y. Cake (www.nycake.com)
Crystal Colors™ (www.sugarpaste.com)

Ingredients

Confectioners' and granulated sugar
Domino® (www.dominosugar.com)

Vanilla beans and extracts
Beanilla® (www.beanilla.com)

Flour
King Arthur® (www.kingarthurflour.com)

Spices, including cardamom
My Spice Sage (www.myspicesage.com)

Packaging

Bakery boxes, cello bags and tissue paper
Nashville Wraps® (www.nashvillewraps.com)

Shipping boxes, heat sealers and packaging material
ULINE® (www.uline.com)

Templates

All templates are supplied at 100%, so there is no need to enlarge.

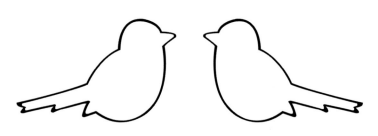

Birds and Filigree, p. 51

Ocean, p. 54

Brush Embroidered Flower, p. 102

Filigree, p. 49

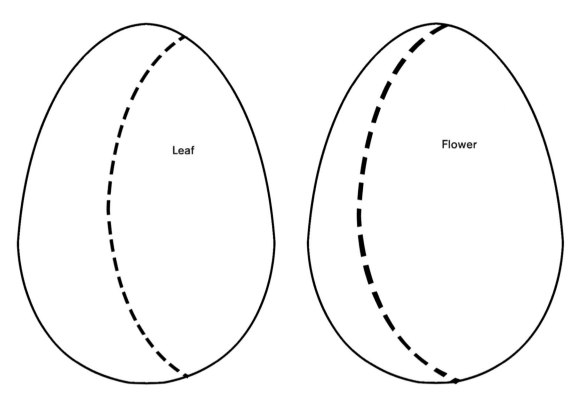

Leaf

Flower

Hyacinth Cookie Pops, p. 41

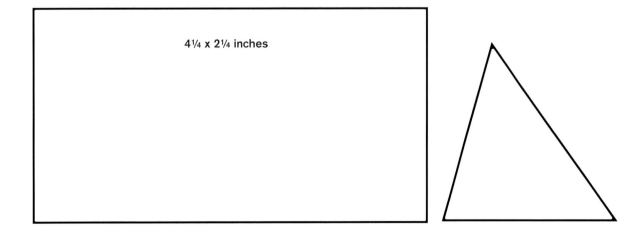

4¼ x 2¼ inches

Place Card Cookies, p. 79

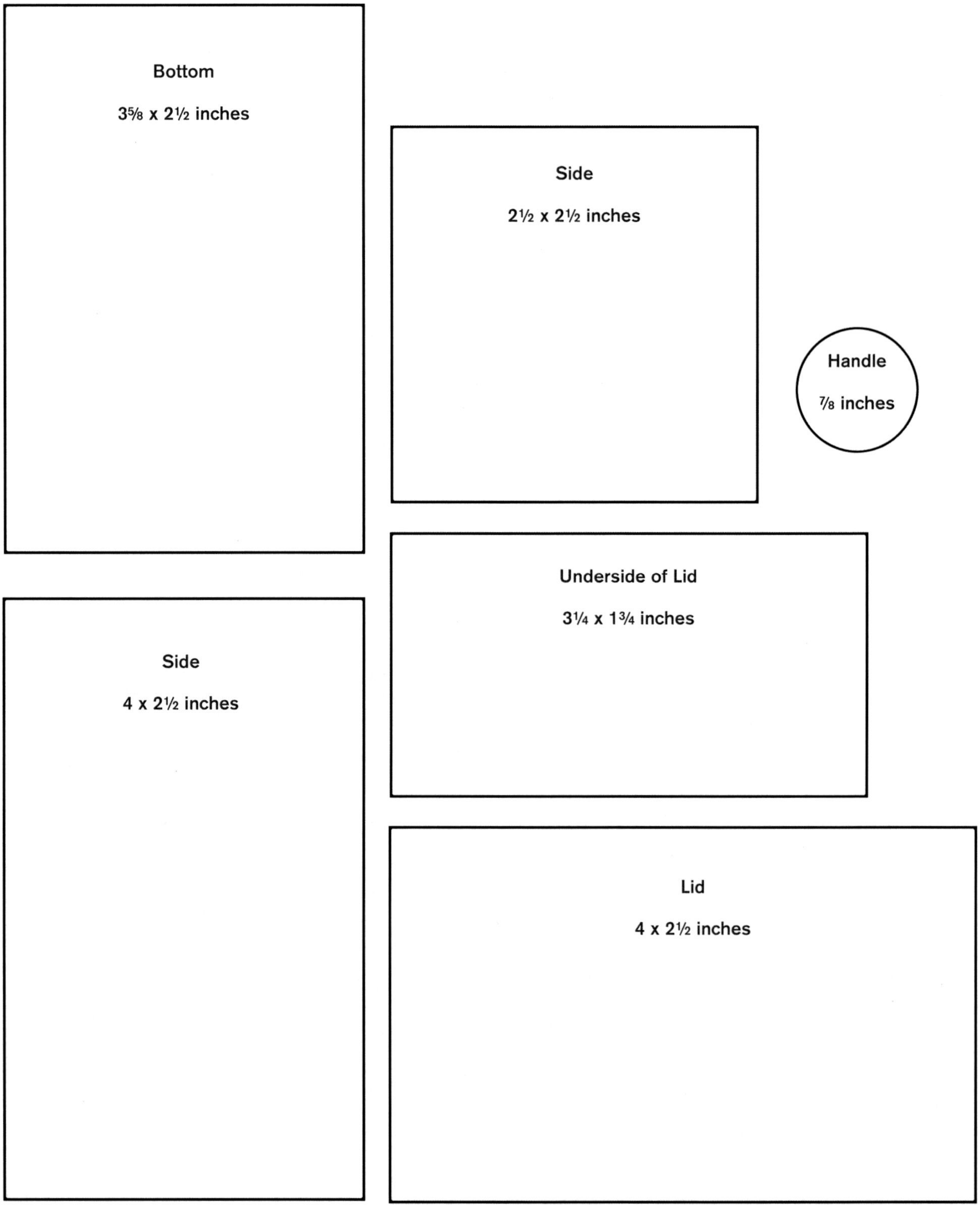

Bottom

3⅝ x 2½ inches

Side

2½ x 2½ inches

Handle

⅞ inches

Side

4 x 2½ inches

Underside of Lid

3¼ x 1¾ inches

Lid

4 x 2½ inches

Cookie Box, p. 57

Tea Set Cookies, p. 105

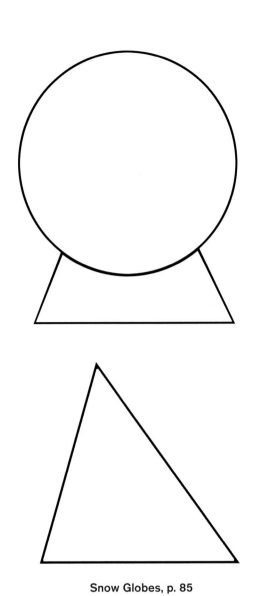

Snow Globes, p. 85

Index

Index

APPENDIX